10/10

MW01048169

20
USA Today
Almanac
for Kids
11

News

Travel

Money

Sports

Life

Tech

Weather

2011

USA Today
Almanac
for Kids 2011

STERLING INNOVATION
An imprint of Sterling Publishing Co., Inc.

New York / London
www.sterlingpublishing.com/kids

ACKNOWLEDGMENTS

Thank you to Ashley, Tommy, Mom, Dad, Elizabeth, Catherine and Carrie for all of your wonderful help! And to Isabel and Max, all the love in the world.

10 9 8 7 6 5 4 3 2 1
6/10

Published by Sterling Publishing Co., Inc.
387 Park Avenue South, New York, NY 10016
© 2010 by Sterling Publishing Co., Inc.
Distributed in Canada by Sterling Publishing
c/o Canadian Manda Group, 165 Dufferin Street
Toronto, Ontario, Canada M6K 3H6
Distributed in the United Kingdom by GMC Distribution Services
Castle Place, 166 High Street, Lewes, East Sussex, England BN7 1XU
Distributed in Australia by Capricorn Link (Australia) Pty. Ltd.
P.O. Box 704, Windsor, NSW 2756, Australia

Cover and interior design by: Ohioboy Art & Design / www.ohioboy.com
Cover images: All cover photos are the property of *USA TODAY*, except *Tyannosaurus Rex*, *World Globe*, *Weather Vane*, *Bald Eagle*, *Cheetah*: Shutterstock; Astronaut: *NASA*; Michelle Obama (back cover): Offical White House Photo by Samantha Appleton

Printed in China
All rights reserved

Sterling ISBN 978-1-4027-7047-0

For information about custom editions, special sales, premium and corporate purchases, please contact Sterling Special Sales Department at 800-805-5489 or specialsales@sterlingpublishing.com.

USA
TODAY.
usatoday.com

Contents

OSCAR

VEGGIES

Olympics

EQUALITY

Anne Frank

WELCOME TO Fabulous LAS VEGAS NEVADA

Introduction

For nearly three decades, USA TODAY has covered the stories that have gripped us as a nation, including the Challenger disaster, the September 11 attacks, the death of Princess Diana, the devastation and aftermath of Hurricane Katrina, and the election of Barack Obama.

In any given day we might report on the big new video game, the newest hit TV show, and the brightest new star in Hollywood; or we might interview the president, report on the best place to put your money, and provide weight-loss inspiration.

One reason we're proud to partner with Sterling Publishing on this almanac is that you'll find useful information on everything from creating a healthful environment in your home to the latest policies in stem-cell research to the top 10 books for young adults. In this almanac you can learn about the countries of the world, the states in the nation, and people making differences in their local communities.

In the words of USA TODAY's founder, Al Neuharth, we've tried to reflect "the good and the bad, the glad and the sad." Another reason we're proud to partner with Sterling Publishing is that this almanac covers some of the good news that's happening in this country. Whether it's kids making a difference, celebrities helping the homeless, or scientists racing to find cures to terrible diseases, this almanac celebrates those who make a difference. At USA TODAY we think that's important. You can read more inspiring stories at kindness.usatoday.com.

At USA TODAY we're also known for our graphics. In this book you'll see a stunning array of photographs—celebrities, animals, sports, and landscapes. Many of these were taken by our talented USA TODAY photographers. You'll also see some of our USA TODAY Snapshots, which appear on the front pages of our four newspaper sections. They are a creative way to give a sense of the statistics that shape our nation and are the work of our talented researchers and designers.

You'll also find USA TODAY stories mixed throughout this book. Whether it's an article about Miley Cyrus, stem-cell research, or the Super Bowl, our USA TODAY newsroom gathers the best information and presents it in a way that's informative and enjoyable.

USA TODAY was founded nearly 30 years ago with this mission:

USA TODAY hopes to serve as a forum for better understanding and unity to help make the USA truly one nation.

One last reason we're proud of this almanac: better understanding and unity require information. This almanac has great information on a range of topics. We hope you enjoy it.

—The Editors of USA TODAY

➜ *Quick Look*

NEWSMAKERS 2009

↑ BARACK OBAMA AND JOE BIDEN

↑ OPRAH WINFREY

↑ TIMOTHY GEITHNER

CHESLEY B. SULLENBERGER ↑

↑ BERNIE MADOFF

↑ SARAH PALIN AND JOHN McCAIN

← JAMES CAMERON

↓ MICHAEL JACKSON

• The 2008 U.S. presidential race was an historic event from start to finish, beginning with the leading candidates for the democratic nomination: female **Senator Hillary Clinton** and African-American **Senator Barack H. Obama**. The excitement continued when republican **Senator John McCain** chose female Alaskan **Governor Sarah Palin** to be his running mate, and then culminated in the momentous election of Senator Barack H. Obama as the first African-American president of the United States.

• **Pilot Captain Chesley "Sully" Sullenberger** became a national hero in January, 2009. After his U.S. Airways Flight 1549 was struck by geese, Sullenberger calmly and bravely glided the jet to safety on the waters of the Hudson River and saved the lives of everyone aboard.

• In March 2009, former financier **Bernie Madoff** was convicted as the perpetrator of the largest ponzi scheme ever lead by a single person. Countless individual victims, along with many charities and universities, fell prey to his multi-billion dollar scam.

CONAN O'BRIEN AND JAY LENO ↑

• In 2008, the **U.S. economy** suffered its most significant downturn since the Great Depression of the 1930s. Experts predict the recovery will take many years. **Timothy Geithner**'s role as secretary of the treasury includes directing the federal government's economic response.

• The classic late-night talk show *The Tonight Show*, which was hosted by **Johnny Carson** from 1962 until 1992 and then **Jay Leno** until 2009, got a brief infusion of youthful energy in late-night funny guy **Conan O'Brien**, only to have Jay Leno return as host eight months later.

• Oprah Winfrey, host of the highest-rated, longest-running and most influential talk show in the history of American television, announced on November 19, 2009, that her beloved show would be ending on Sept. 9, 2011, after 25 seasons on the air.

• Twelve years after releasing *Titanic*, currently the highest grossing film in the world, director **James Cameron** released his ground-breaking *Avatar*, composed of computer generated animation—with which he will no doubt continue to shatter box-office records.

↑ HILLARY CLINTON

• We lost some of our most beloved celebrity icons—national treasures who had become significant representations of a certain time in our lives and a permanent part of the fabric of American history—including: Ted Kennedy, Walter Cronkite, **Michael Jackson**, Farrah Fawcett, and Patrick Swayze.

HOT YOUNG CELEBRITIES

RAFAEL NADAL ↑

TAYLOR SWIFT ↑

↑ LeBRON JAMES

JUSTIN TIMBERLAKE ↑

↑ ZAC EFFRON

↑ DANIEL RADCLIFFE

↑ RIHANNA

KANYE WEST ↑

↑ MILEY CYRUS

JONAS BROTHERS ↑

↑ ROBERT PATTINSON

↓ SHIA LeBEOUF

DAKOTA FANNING ↑

KRISTEN STEWART ↑

Animals

THE KINGDOMS OF LIFE

In order for scientists to keep an organized record of the many different species, traits, and relationships of animals, they follow a system of classification with multiple levels. Created by the Swedish naturalist Carolus Linnaeus (1707–78), this system separates both plants and animals by physical similarities and identifies each species with its own name.

This method of categorization, called **taxonomy**, gives a clear structure to the complex world of plants and animals, full of seemingly infinite variety. Every living creature belongs to one of the five **kingdoms of life**:

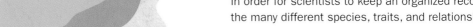

Within the animal kingdom, there are several more specific levels of classification, so each animal can be accurately described and understood according to its various characteristics. The one trait that initially distinguishes every single animal throughout history and places it squarely into one of two clear groups— **vertebrates** and **invertebrates**—is whether they have a backbone.

These two groups are then subdivided into more specific groups, called **phyla**, that organize animals according to the general makeup of their body, both inside and out. Next comes an animal's **class**, which has to do with how an animal's body operates. After the class division come the increasingly more specific categories of **order**, **family**, and **genus**, until we arrive at the final and most specific level in the animal kingdom: the **species** to which an animal belongs.

THE FIVE KINGDOMS OF LIFE

1. **MONERA:** one-celled bacteria with no nucleus

2. **PROTISTA:** one-celled bacteria that do a have a nucleus, such as amoebas

3. **FUNGI:** stationary beings containing more than one cell, with nuclei, that must receive all food from outside sources, such as molds and mushrooms

4. **PLANTS:** stationary, many-celled organisms that engage in photosynthesis to feed themselves, including trees, flowers, fruits and vegetables

5. **ANIMALS:** a complex array of multicellular creatures that can move on their own and must rely on outside sources of food

HAVE YOU HEARD?

Out of all the species of animals in the world (more than 15 million), at least 95 percent of them are invertebrates!

VERTEBRATES

BACKBONE

FISH: Fish are cold-blooded animals who breathe through gills. Scales cover their bodies, and they must remain in water in order to survive. Except for sharks, who give birth to their young, fish reproduce by laying eggs. Fish include everything from the little household goldfish to the great white shark.

AMPHIBIANS: Amphibians, also cold-blooded, lay their eggs in water and breathe through gills while immersed, but they are able to survive on both land and water. Frogs breathe through lungs while on land, while some other amphibians are able to breathe through their skin. Amphibians include frogs, toads, and salamanders.

RED EYED TREE FROG

REPTILES: Reptiles are also scaly, cold-blooded animals who can live either on land or in water. Their primary mode of reproduction involves laying eggs. Reptiles include lizards, turtles, snakes, alligators, and crocodiles.

LIZARD

OWL

BIRDS: Birds are warm-blooded animals with feathers and wings instead of scales. They all lay eggs and breathe through lungs, and most species of birds (aside from penguins and ostriches) can fly. Birds include owls, eagles, sparrows, ducks, and parrots.

MAMMALS: Mammals are warm-blooded animals who breathe through lungs and, with the exception of dolphins, whales and porpoises, who live in water, are covered in fur or hair. They give live birth to their young (except for the platypus and mammal mothers breastfeed their babies. Mammals include pandas, lions, elephants, apes, and dogs.)

ORANGUTAN

INVERTEBRATES

BACKBONE

WATER SPONGES: Sponges live in water, where they cannot move on their own but attach to rocks, shells, or coral.

SPONGE

CNIDARIA: Cnidaria live in water, with tentacles that surround the mouth at one end of their body, through which they eat and eliminate waste. Cnidaria include coral, jellyfish, and Portuguese man-of-war.

ECHINODERMS: Echinoderms are marine animals who live in the sea. Their skeletons exist on the outside of their bodies. Echinoderms include sand dollars, sea urchins, and sea stars.

JELLYFISH

WORMS: Worms, that can live almost anywhere including within other living animals, have a fluid-filled body inside muscle and a tough skin. Worms include earthworms, roundworms, and flatworms.

MOLLUSKS: Mollusks, some of the first animals ever to live on the earth, can live either on land or in the sea. They have soft bodies that are often protected by a hard outside shell. Mollusks include snails, slugs, oysters, clams, octopuses, and squid.

COMMON ATLANTIC OCTOPUS

ARTHROPODS: Arthropods, like Echinoderms, have exoskeletons, but their exterior skeletons have many segments and joints, allowing for a far wider range of movement. Arthropod groups include insects (the only invertebrates who can fly, such as ants, bees, and butterflies), arachnids (spiders and scorpions), myriapods (centipedes and millipedes), and crustaceans (lobsters, shrimp, and crab).

SPINY LOBSTER

DINOSAURS FOREVER

The excitement never ends for dinosaur fans: In July 2009, three previously unknown species of dinosaurs were discovered from fossils dug up in Queensland, Australia. Two were herbivores, both around 52 feet long, one resembling a giraffe-like creature and the other shaped more like a hippopotamus. The third species, a 1,100-pound carnivore nicknamed Banjo by the paleontologists who found him, was a fast and treacherous predator, reminiscent of the frightening velociraptor (remember those from the *Jurassic Park* movies?), only far larger. The fossils discovered were an incredible 98 million years old.

A discovery like this is a dream come true for a paleontologist, something you might think may never happen again. However, Peter Dodson of the University of Pennsylvania and Steve Wang of Swarthmore College estimate that 71 percent of all dinosaur genera—groups of dinosaur species— have yet to be discovered. Dodson assures people that "it's a safe bet that a child born today could expect a very fruitful career in dinosaur paleontology."

ENDANGERED SPECIES

The Endangered Species Act—passed in 1973, amended regularly to reflect new approaches, and still regarded as the world's most effective wildlife conservation law—exists to protect plant and animal species

BROWN BEAR

from disappearing from the earth forever. Its goal, as stated in the Endangered Species Bulletin of November/December 1999, is an ambitious one: "to reverse the alarming trend of human-caused extinctions that threaten the ecosystems we all share." When we think about species that are in danger, from the tiniest beetle to the great blue whale, it's vital to remember that saving them involves far more than just the protection of each individual species—habitats and environments where the species live and interact are just as important and as in danger as the species themselves.

Some Animals on the Endangered Species List of the U.S. Fish and Wildlife Service

blue whale	jaguar
brown bear	leopard
cheetah	ocelot
cougar	red wolf
giant panda	Steller sea lion
gray wolf	tiger

GIANT PANDA

TIGERS ENDANGERED

TIGERS ENDANGERED

Did you know that there are fewer than 5,000 tigers left in the world? And that this number continues to decrease? We are in danger of losing one of the most majestic and mythologized animals in existence. Luckily, Tigers Forever (tigersforever.org) is an exciting initiative—established in 2008 with the support of the Panthera Wildlife Trust and the Wildlife Conservation Society—committed to saving the world's wild tigers.

Its goal is to increase the population of tigers in regions across Asia by 50 percent within 10 years. Its plan requires supporters in government, business, and wildlife conservation groups across the world. The key tiger sites they are targeting are Cambodia, China, India, Indonesia, Laos, Myanmar, the Russian Far East, and Thailand.

BLUE WHALE

HAVE YOU HEARD?

The blue whale is by far the largest known animal to have ever lived. Blue whales can grow to 200 tons, which is 400,000 pounds!

CHEETAH

OSTRICH

PEREGRINE FALCON

WHALE SHARK

CROCODILE

BEE HUMMINGBIRD

RECORD BREAKERS:

Fastest:

FASTEST LAND MAMMAL, SHORT DISTANCES: cheetah at 70 mph

 The fastest human being, Usain Bolt from Jamaica, runs short distances at a breathtaking speed of 23.35 mph

FASTEST LAND MAMMAL, LONG DISTANCES: pronghorn or American antelope at 35 mph for 4 hrs

FASTEST HUNTING BIRD: peregrine falcon dives at 200 mph

FASTEST FLYING BIRD: racing pigeon at about 100 mph

FASTEST RUNNING BIRD: ostrich at 43 mph

FASTEST DOG: greyhound at 45 mph

FASTEST MARINE MAMMALS: Dall's porpoise and killer whales, at 55 mph

FASTEST FISH: cosmopolitan sailfish at 68 mph

 Olympics swimming champion Michael Phelps can swim at speeds up to 4.34 mph

FASTEST FLYING INSECT: dragonfly at 35 mph

FASTEST RUNNING INSECT: cockroach at 3 mph

COCKROACH

Largest:

LARGEST LAND MAMMAL: African bush elephant at 13 feet high and 8 tons

LARGEST FLYING BIRD: great bustard at 32 pounds and 4 ft. long

LARGEST AND TALLEST BIRD ON LAND: ostrich at 9 ft. tall and 345 lbs.

LARGEST MARINE MAMMAL: blue whale averages 110 feet long and 209 tons

LARGEST FISH: whale shark at 41 ft., 6 in. long

LONGEST KNOWN ANIMAL: arctic lion's mane jellyfish, with a bell (body) 7 ft., 6 in. in diameter and tentacles up to 120 ft. long

LARGEST REPTILE: saltwater crocodile at 16 ft. long and 1,150 lbs.

LARGEST LIZARD: Komodo dragon at 9–10 ft. long and up to 300 lbs.

LARGEST SNAKE: reticulated python, at 26–32 ft. long

LARGEST INSECT: stick insect at 15 ft. long

Smallest:

SMALLEST MAMMAL: bumblebee bat at 1.1–1.3 in.

SMALLEST BIRD: bee hummingbird at 1–2 in. long and .06 oz.

SMALLEST BREED OF DOG: chihuahua

SMALLEST SNAKE: thread snake at under 4 in. long

SMALLEST FISH: *Paydocypris progenetica* (carp family) at .3 in. long

SMALLEST REPTILE: Jaragua dwarf gecko at .6 in. long

SMALLEST INSECT: fairyfly at .01 in. long

AFRICAN BUSH ELEPHANT

WHY DON'T CHIMPANZEES MAKE GOOD PETS?

JANE GOODALL

Chimpanzees can be very cute and human-like. You can find them featured in movies and television commercials, smiling, clapping, wearing cute outfits, shaking hands, and even driving cars. But in 2009, when the popular, mediagenic 200-pound chimp named Travis brutally mauled a friend and frequent visitor of his owner, the world was issued a painful reminder that, no matter how cute, chimpanzees do not make good pets.

Jane Goodall, one of the world's foremost experts on chimpanzees, who is most famous for her study of their social interactions in the wild (in Tanzania) and for the Jane Goodall Institute, which is dedicated to the research and protection of chimpanzees, has been telling us this for decades.

First of all, she warns, they are far stronger than humans. By age five, they are stronger than most human adults, and in adulthood, they become at least five times as strong (in captivity they tend to live between 50 and 60 years).

In addition (unless they are housed in a sanctuary or top-quality zoo), no matter how adorable and dependent they are as youngsters, the time will inevitably come when chimpanzees will grow dissatisfied and need to leave their owners. At some point, Goodall asserts on her Web site, janegoodall.org, they "become destructive and resentful of discipline. They can, and will, bite."

Unfortunately, once they have spent time being raised in a human environment, they can no longer return to their African home, nor will most zoos accept them back. This means that, historically, many well-loved pet chimps wound up in medical research laboratories; today, they are more likely to end up in a shabby roadside zoo.

So as we appreciate their precocious cuteness, let's do it from the safe proximity of high-quality zoos or a nature channel on TV.

ANIMAL RIGHTS ORGANIZATIONS

The **ASPCA** (American Society for the Prevention of Cruelty to Animals) was the first humane society established in North America and has grown to become one of the largest and most influential in the world. Founded by Henry Bergh in 1866, the work of the ASPCA is inspired by the understanding that animals are "entitled to kind and respectful treatment at the hands of humans, and must be protected under the law." For more information see the Web site aspca.org.

PETA (People for the Ethical Treatment of Animals), founded in 1980, has become the largest animal rights organization in the world, with more than 2 million members and supporters. It works under the basic principle that "animals are not ours to eat, wear, experiment on, or use for entertainment" and focuses its attention on the four areas it has determined that the most animals suffer most intensely: factory farms, laboratories, the clothing trade, and the entertainment industry. For more information, see the Web site peta.org.

BISCUIT

"ORDINARY" PETS TO THE RESCUE

Most of the time, Biscuit the bulldog is just a regular stubby-legged young dude who runs around the yard collecting sticks and making everyone laugh with his goofy antics. But each Friday, once he dons his green work vest, he adjusts his jowly mug into an expression of genial concern, discards all thoughts of canine capers, and calmly sets about the business of cheering up stroke patients or encouraging children in their classrooms.

"This is his calling," said his owner, Shannon Pryor, 28, of Wheat Ridge, Denver. She recognized Biscuit's highly empathetic nature when he was a wee pup and she was convalescing with a broken foot. Pryor got herself and Biscuit registered as a pet therapy team through Denver Pet Partners when he was one year old, and now they spend Friday mornings at either a stroke rehabilitation center or a nearby elementary school.

Across the country, thousands of pets and their owners are spending time with the infirm, the depressed, or the distressed, as well as with legions of children and adults in difficult straits who get a boost from the unconditional acceptance and cheerful demeanor of an animal.

Therapy dogs, as they are known, are not service dogs, who go through years of specialized training to assist people who have disabilities. Therapy dogs are house pets with a special affinity for people, a placid demeanor, and solid, reliable obedience skills. The ability of these animals to motivate, cheer, stabilize, and calm people has begun to be widely publicized in recent years. Now, doctors, counselors, teachers, librarians, physical therapists, and crisis managers are so convinced of the positive power of animals that they're lining up to request teams to spend healing time with people in their charge.

The pet-owning public is responding in ever-burgeoning numbers. Nationwide, large pet-training programs are reporting more than 10,000 or even 15,000 registered animal therapy teams. Thousands more people and pets are registered with smaller groups or simply do their thing without group affiliation.

Cats and birds get into the act

With each passing month, the whole pet therapy arena seems to evolve:

- Dogs aren't the only species being used. Cats, llamas, miniature horses, rabbits, and birds have been trained and registered.

- Dozens of new applications are being tried. Therapy animals are frequenting schools to help with reading programs or with special-education students, funeral homes to comfort survivors, disaster sites to help quell the chaos, and prisons to offer nonjudgmental friendship. The U.S. military sent the first therapy dogs to a war zone in December 2007 to help the troops in Iraq.

Contrary to popular belief, there's no ideal breed for this sort of volunteer work. "They can be 3 pounds to 150 pounds, of any breed," Delta Society's JoAnn Turnbull says. Some dogs have disabilities, and "30 percent of the dogs we register are from shelters or rescue groups."

CHANGING THEIR LIVES FOR THE LOVE OF ANIMALS

The important roles that YouTube and the Internet play in the lives of teenagers seem to be having a surprising effect: a rise in adolescent vegetarianism.

Vegetarianism has a wide range of definitions, from a diet that primarily excludes red meat and may contain some fish or poultry to veganism, which is an avoidance of all animal products, including eggs and diary. Using a broad understanding of the term, the federal Centers for Disease Control and Prevention has estimated that at least 367,000 kids avoid eating meat, which is about 1 in 200.

In most cases, it is animal welfare rather than personal health that is driving teenagers to make these decisions, and this is where the Internet comes in. Anecdotally, we are learning that the animal-slaughter videos on YouTube and other information to be found on the Internet are having a strong impact on the developing sensibilities of kids.

Nicole Nightingale, a teenager from Safety Harbor, Florida, was researching chickens on the Internet when she discovered a video on YouTube that showed the birds being slaughtered. At the end, viewers were invited to go to the Web site peta.org—People for the Ethical Treatment of Animals.

Nicole decided to go vegan. Her parents were skeptical at first, but it ended up working out so well that her mother eventually took steps to become a vegetarian as well. Nicole believes her experience was typical for a preadolescent vegetarian. "A lot more kids are using the Internet. They're curious about stuff and trying to become independent, and they're trying to find out who they are," she said.

Eating vegetarian can be a very healthy lifestyle if done with care, but it involved more than simply cutting out meat and filling up on pasta or French fries. It's always healthy to eat lots of fruits and vegetables, but teens must also be sure to consume sufficient amounts of protein, vitamins B12 and D, iron, calcium, and other important nutrients that most people get from meat, eggs, and dairy.

USA TODAY Snapshots®

The pet story

Total number of pets owned in the USA (in millions):

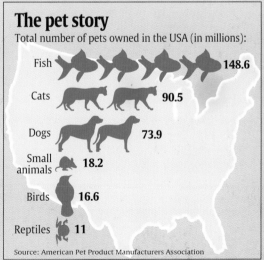

Fish	148.6
Cats	90.5
Dogs	73.9
Small animals	18.2
Birds	16.6
Reptiles	11

Source: American Pet Product Manufacturers Association

By David Stuckey and Marcy E. Mullins, USA TODAY

BODY SYSTEMS

The circulatory system involves a selection of organs designed to channel blood throughout the body. The **heart** pumps the blood through the **arteries** that transport it, along with the necessary oxygen and nutrients it contains. Through blood vessels called **capillaries**, the cells receive the nourishment they need, giving off carbon dioxide and other waste. **Veins** then carry the blood back to the heart, keeping the waste away from the cells and carrying it to the organs that will dispose of it. → → → → → → → → → → → → → → →

VEINS

HEART

The digestive system is in charge of breaking down food into the vitamins, minerals, carbohydrates, proteins, and fats required to nourish body. Once it is eaten, food passes through the **esophagus** to the stomach, where stomach acids begin to digest it. From there, the food travels into the **small intestine**, where enzymes, bile, and insulin break it down into nutrients and water ready to continue through the **large intestine** and be absorbed into the bloodstream. The undigested food that isn't used becomes waste and is eliminated from the body.

The immune system works to keep the body healthy and protect it against infections and diseases. Organs, tissues, blood cells, and cell products work together to fight against dangerous external organisms. The **anatomic response**, involving the **tonsils**, the **adenoids**, and **mucous membranes**, among other things, physically blocks or traps certain outside substances that may enter the body. The **inflammatory system** can eliminate harmful substances from the body through actions such as coughing, sneezing, and fever. In what is called the **immune response, white blood cells** work with the **lymph nodes** to produce **antibodies**, which fight bacteria, viruses, and other **antigens**. The **thymus** and the **spleen** also play important roles in the body's complicated defense system against bacteria and disease.

BLOOD CELLS

The endocrine system is made up of **glands** that produce **hormones**, chemicals that move through the bloodstream and control various functions of the body. Called the body's messengers, these hormones contribute to the body's growth, metabolism, sleep, and sexual development, among other functions.

GLANDS

The integumentary system is made up of **skin**, **hair**, **nails**, **sense receptors**, **sweat glands**, and **oil glands**. It is the protector of the body from the outside environment, acting as a barrier; a sensory system that alerts the brain to various feelings such as heat, cold, and pain; and a reactor that follows the brain's instructions (such as to produce sweat to cool the body when needed).

The lymphatic system supports a body's immune response by producing **white blood cells** and the **antibodies** that fight disease. **Lymph nodes** produce a liquid called **lymph**, which is distributed throughout tissues and the bloodstream via a collaboration of **vessels**, delivering nutrients to the cells and ridding them of bacteria and excess fluid.

The muscular system includes three different types of muscles. **Skeletal muscles**—the muscles we can see—are attached to the bones and help the body move. These are the only muscles under our direct control. **Smooth muscles** are found inside organs, including the digestive system and air passages, and do their work automatically, controlled by other systems of the body. **Cardiac muscles**, also involuntary, pump blood through the heart to the body.

The nervous system includes the **brain** and the **spinal cord** (the central nervous system) and **neurons** throughout the body (the peripheral nervous system). The brain works to control the other systems by sending signals via the spinal cord as **nerve impulses** throughout the body, telling muscles and organs what to do and commanding everything from thought, speech, and movement to the various internal bodily systems.

The reproductive system generates **sperm cells** in men and **egg cells** in women. Sperm fertilizes the egg, or **ovum**, in a woman's **fallopian tube**, and the fertilized egg then moves to the **uterus**, where it becomes an embryo, then a fetus, and eventually a baby.

EAT SMART

What you eat can have a huge impact on how well your brain functions. Brain expert and bestselling author Daniel Amen, MD, gives his patients and readers many useful tips for keeping their brain healthy, including these:

- Drink enough water and healthy, sugar-free liquids to stay hydrated—your brain is 80 percent water!
- Be sure to get enough omega-3 fatty acids (good fat) to feed the important fat in your brain from food such as fish and flax seed and from supplements as well.
- Eat a diet rich in antioxidants from fruits and vegetables, such as berries, plums, broccoli, avocados, and red bell peppers, among others, to protect your brain from deterioration.

HAVE YOU HEARD?

We lose between 30,000 and 40,000 skin cells every single minute, but the human skin constantly renews itself, so we don't need to worry that it will wear away.

LUNGS

The respiratory system is responsible for bringing air into the body, absorbing the **oxygen** we need and expelling the **carbon dioxide** we don't. After entering the body through the nose or mouth, air travels down the **trachea** (the windpipe), through two tubes called **bronchi**, and into the **lungs**. Once there, the tubes divide into many smaller tubes and then into **alveoli**, tiny air cells that allow oxygen to enter the bloodstream, while carbon dioxide is sent back into the lungs and exhaled.

The skeletal system is made up of the **bones**, **ligaments**, **tendons**, **joints**, and **cartilage** that support the body, give it its shape, and work with the muscular system to help it move. The bones also protect internal organs, store minerals such as calcium, and produce red and white blood cells in the fatty tissue called **marrow** contained inside.

The urinary system removes waste from the body. In the **kidneys**, waste and toxins are cleansed from the blood and combined with water. This liquid then moves through two tubes called **ureters** into the **bladder**, after which it is eliminated from the body through the **urethra**, as **urine**.

KIDNEYS

5 THE FIVE SENSES

Your five senses—hearing, sight, smell, taste and touch—are the way you receive information about the world around you. They help you seek things that are important for you, such as food or warmth in the cold, and protect yourself from things that have the potential to be dangerous, such as fire or a poisonous plant.

sight: Vision is a complicated sense, involving many elements working together to form what is described as **visual perception**. First, light waves travel through the **pupil** to hit the **lens** and **cornea**, where shapes and colors are determined. These light waves then reach the **retina**, a membrane at the back of the eye, where they are converted into patterns of neural impulses that move along the **optic nerve** to the brain, where they are perceived as images. The translations of these nerve impulses into images that occur in the brain are as vital to our experience of sight as the actions of our eyes.

hearing: Similar to the process of visual perception, hearing involves the movement of sound (rather than light) waves from the outside, this time through the ear, where they are turned into nerve impulses and interpreted by the brain. The sound vibrations enter through the **outer ear** that we see and travel to the **eardrum**. The resulting vibrations of the eardrum move three little bones in the **middle ear,** which are detected by tiny hairs on the **auditory nerve** in the **inner ear**, which then turns them into neural impulses and sends them on to the brain.

taste: Our sense of taste starts with the **taste buds** that cover the surface of the tongue, and can also be found on the roof of the mouth and in the throat. The four primary taste sensations have traditionally been understood to be **sweet**, **sour**, **salty** and **bitter**. However, scientists have begun to add a fifth taste to this list: *umami*, which is Japanese for savory. Of course, foods come in a far richer variety of flavors beyond these five tastes, and that is where the sense of smell comes in. Taste and smell signals work together in the same part of the brain, and most of what is perceived as taste is actually a result of these two senses working in tandem.

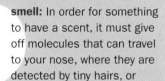

smell: In order for something to have a scent, it must give off molecules that can travel to your nose, where they are detected by tiny hairs, or **cilia**, on nerve cells called **olfactory receptors**. The chemicals are then passed as electrical impulses to the brain, where they are perceived as smell. The olfactory bulb is part of the **limbic system**, a portion of the brain that is the seat of human emotions, which is why smells tend to trigger certain memories and emotional responses.

touch: Through your sense of touch, you can feel heat, cold, pain, itch and pressure, all via millions of different nerve receptors in the **epidermis** and the **dermis**, two layers of skin covering the body. Every touch you feel, from the lightest tickle to a painful pinch, creates nerve signals that are sent to the brain for quick interpretation and reaction.

DAIRY (1–2 servings a day) OR VITAMIN D/CALCIUM SUPPLEMENTS

NUTS, SEEDS, BEANS & TOFU   FISH, POULTRY & EGGS

VEGETABLES & FRUITS   HEALTHY FATS/OILS   WHOLE GRAINS

DAILY EXERCISE & WEIGHT CONTROL

THE HEALTHY EATING PYRAMID

The faculty in the Department of Nutrition at the Harvard School of Public Health have created a new food pyramid, based on current science and with a clear focus on a healthy diet and lifestyle. While this food pyramid and the tips that accompany it are designed for adults, not kids, they can provide great direction for a nutritious diet for the whole family.

The five "Quick Tips" they give on their Web site are the following:

1. Begin with exercise: a healthy diet must always include regular exercise.

2. Use the pyramid as a guide to what to eat when you eat—more foods from the bottom of the pyramid, and fewer from the top.

3. Fill your diet with plants, including fruits, vegetables, and whole grains.

4. Cut down on unhealthy "staples" of the American diet, including red meat, white flour, sweet drinks, and fatty snacks.

5. Be sure to include a multivitamin supplement.

The Harvard Healthy Eating Pyramid is something you can show your parents, for them to follow and be inspired by as they plan your family's diet. The set up of the pyramid starts at the bottom, with Daily Exercise and Weight Control taking up the widest spot on the pyramid. Next up comes the foods of which people should eat the most: Vegetables & Fruits, Healthy Fats/Oils, and Whole Grains. Following that is a section for Nuts, Seeds, Beans & Tofu and Fish, Poulty & Eggs. In the next to last spot is Diary (1–2 servings a day) or Vitamin D/Calcium supplements, and at the very top, in the smallest spot on the pyramid, sits Red Meat & Butter, Refined Grains, Sugary and Salty items. Serving amounts can vary for kids versus adults, but the positions—such as placing fruits, vegetables and exercise in much more important positions than red meat and sugary snacks—apply to healthy diets for all ages.

WHY DO WE EXERCISE?

We all know that exercise is a vital component of a healthy lifestyle and is necessary to keep us fit, make us strong, and prolong our lives. But it's important to remember how much exercise affects our mental and emotional health as well. In addition to being a terrific stress reliever, exercise also releases endorphins and other chemicals that improve our moods. It makes us feel and look better physically, think more clearly, and is scientifically proven to make us happier. Luckily, there are so many different ways to bring exercise into our lives, so we can all find something we actually enjoy—at least most of the time. And we all have time to make ourselves happy, don't we?

HAVE YOU HEARD?

Obesity—the state of being 30 or more pounds over a healthy weight—cost the United States an estimated $147 billion in weight-related medical bills in 2008, double what it was a decade ago. The yearly medical bills of obese patients are more than $1,300 higher than those of patients who are at more healthy weights.

CREATE A HEALTHFUL ENVIRONMENT IN YOUR HOME

Kids can take charge and work with their parents to improve the food and clean up the physical activity environment in their homes, says David Ludwig, director of the Optimal Weight for Life Program at Children's Hospital in Boston. He and his staff have treated more than 5,000 overweight children. He knows losing weight is a struggle for many families.

His suggestions:

1. **Stock up on good food**
   Fill your house with foods that are both delicious and nutritious (fruits, vegetables, whole grains, nuts, beans, fish, lean protein, reduced-fat dairy products) and don't bring home junk food.

2. **Make sweets a treat**
   Save treats for special occasions. You don't have to give up sweets entirely, but go out for them instead of having them at home, he says.

3. **Ditch the drive-through**
   Avoid fast food, he says. Ludwig did a study that showed overweight teens consume about 400 more calories on a day when they consume fast food compared with a day in which they don't.

4. **Turn off the TV**
   Make physical activity the focus of the home instead of television. Don't allow TVs in the kitchen or bedrooms.

5. **Equip for exercise**
   Make sure older kids have the basic tools to be active: jump ropes, balls, baseball gloves, Frisbees.

6. **Shake it!**
   Encourage everyone to dance! Dancing is an excellent activity, Ludwig says. "Kids love to dance in a nonjudgmental setting. When they are having fun, they are not thinking about it as exercise."

POWER LUNCHES

Busy kids and parents are always scrambling for good ideas to make easy and healthy bagged lunches. Here, two registered dietitians— Elizabeth Ward and Bonnie Taub-Dix— give suggestions for healthful meals to pack at home.

> **TIP #1:**

Start the day out right with a healthy breakfast. "Children can't make it three or four hours in the morning on just sugary cereal or pastry," says Ward. "At breakfast, I try to make sure my kids get a decent dose of protein (egg, cottage cheese, peanut butter), as well as complex carbohydrates like whole-grain toast or oatmeal, fruit, and dairy, such as skim or 1 percent milk or yogurt." Taub-Dix adds: "Breakfast doesn't have to be elaborate . . . It can be something like mozzarella string cheese on a piece of bread. If you grab a glass of milk, that would be great."

> **TIP #2:**

Pack lunches the night before. "It reduces the chaos in the morning," says Ward.

> **TIP #3:**

Pack what you like! Don't waste time and money packing things you know you won't want to eat. "A big thing with kids is the lunch can't be smelly," says Taub-Dix. "That's why many won't take a can of tuna fish for lunch."

Ward's lunch suggestions

- **A slice of leftover thin-crust cheese pizza**, a peach or pear, 8 ounces of 100 percent fruit juice, and a single-serving bag of low-fat popcorn (already popped).

- **Turkey and cheese roll-ups:** Wrap deli turkey around string cheese. Serve with whole-grain pretzels, carrot sticks, or cherry tomatoes, fruit, and 8 ounces of 1 percent low-fat milk.

- **Bagel sandwich:** Leftover cooked, chopped chicken tossed with grapes and low-fat mayo on a 2-ounce whole-wheat bagel. (You can buy these frozen and keep on hand for lunches.) With a single serving carton of raisins and 8 ounces of 1 percent low-fat milk.

Taub-Dix's lunch suggestions

- **Multigrain bread** with 2 tablespoons of crunchy peanut butter and 1 teaspoon of raspberry jam, melon wedge, and 1 cup of low-fat yogurt.

- **Two slices of raisin bread** with two slices of low-fat mozzarella cheese, fresh sugar snap peas, a banana, a handful of almonds, and 1 cup of skim or 1 percent low-fat milk.

- **A cup of cooked whole-wheat pasta** (cooked the night before) tossed with cubes of grilled chicken, carrots, zucchini, pine nuts, and 2 tablespoons of balsamic vinaigrette dressing. Serve with an individual serving of crushed pineapple in its own juice and 1 cup of skim or 1 percent milk.

EXERCISE VIDEO GAMES

New research shows that exercise video games such as Wii Sports and Dance Dance Revolution boost young peoples' activity levels significantly.

The Wii system, made by Nintendo, is controlled by a wireless remote that translates movements to its "Mii" caricature on screen. In Dance Dance Revolution, from video game maker Konami, players use their feet to hit arrows on the game's dance mat, matching their own steps with arrows set in time to music on screen.

Studies measuring the heart rate and oxygen consumption of kids engaging in a variety of popular *exergames* have found many positive effects. Active video gaming requires far more energy than tradition video gaming and can even raise activity levels enough to meet different health guidelines for exercise.

Still, some experts say exergames won't bring the same results as good old-fashioned exercise. Craig Buschner, a professor of kinesiology at California State University–Chico, says video games should be seen as a tool, but not the only tool, to help kids become more physically active. Children should not use these games in place of an hour of tag or a bike ride in the park, he says.

FOOD AND VITAMINS
You Are What You Eat

USA TODAY Snapshots®

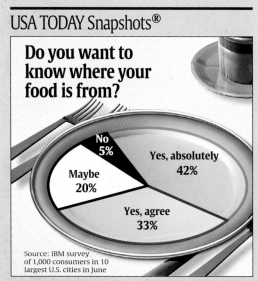

Do you want to know where your food is from?

No 5%
Maybe 20%
Yes, absolutely 42%
Yes, agree 33%

Source: IBM survey of 1,000 consumers in 10 largest U.S. cities in June

By Anne R. Carey and Suzy Parker, USA TODAY

FOOD AND VITAMINS: YOU ARE WHAT YOU EAT

Taking vitamin supplements can help increase your daily intake of vitamins and minerals, but it's important to get a large portion of our vitamins from the foods we eat—from protein, carbohydrates, and fats—as this is when they have the most power (before they are broken down) and the way our bodies can best absorb them. Foods that are a particularly rich source of vitamins and minerals include spinach and other dark leafy greens, broccoli, dark-colored berries, fish, sweet potato, watermelon, tomato and tomato juice, liver, legumes, and others.

Chamomile

Carrot
"Hercules"

Thyme   Mace

Dill

MICHELLE OBAMA

NEW WHITE HOUSE VEGGIE GARDEN

For the first time since First Lady Eleanor Roosevelt planted her "victory garden" during World War II, the White House grounds once again feature a vegetable garden. First Lady Michelle Obama, joined by 26 local fifth graders armed with shovels, rakes, and pitchforks, started work on the 1,100-square-foot organic herb and vegetable plot that includes spinach, broccoli, various lettuces, kale, collard greens, assorted herbs, and even a beehive.

The garden is intended to grow year-round produce for the White House and Miriam's Kitchen, a nearby soup kitchen. The student gardeners, all from nearby Bancroft Elementary School, will be involved in planting crops, tending the garden, and harvesting.

The Obamas are advocates of healthy eating based on fresh, organic meals with loads of vegetables and fruits. "My girls like vegetables more if they taste good," Obama said and added, "Especially if they're involved in planting it and picking it."

Environment & Weather

LAND AND WATER REGIONS OF THE EARTH

FORESTS

Approximately one-third of the earth's land surface excluding Antarctica is covered by different kinds of forests.

Coniferous, or **evergreen**, **forests** exist in areas farthest from the equator and contain primarily cone-bearing trees, including pines, hemlocks, spruces, and firs. Most of these trees, with their softer woods and small leaves or needles, thrive in cold environments, although a few coniferous trees such as cypresses and redwoods can be found in warmer regions. Coniferous forests grow in regions of North America, Scandinavia, Russia, and parts of Asia.

Temperate forests include a wide range of forests that tend in general to have warm summers, cold winters, and lots of rain and snow year round. They include multiple varieties of trees, most of which are deciduous as opposed to evergreen, so they shed their leaves in the autumn and grow new ones each spring. Temperate forests are located in the eastern United States and Canada, northern Europe and Asia, and southern Australia.

Tropical rain forests are generally found closest to the equator. Their lush environments, nourished by warmth and heavy rainfall nearly all year long, house the widest range of plants and animals on the earth. Trees in the rain forest grow to tremendous heights and either keep their leaves year round or lose them at different times. A mature rain forest often has several layers of different trees and plants. The uppermost layer, called the emergent layer, is the tops of the tallest trees, some close to 200 feet tall. Beneath that is the canopy, a rich layer of trees and creatures that flourish in lots of sunlight. Next is the understory, a looser scattering of shorter trees, then a layer of shrubs, and finally the root-laced forest floor, which is almost entirely blocked from sunlight, so not much grows there. Despite the rich diversity of plant and animal life within our world's rain forests—more than half of the plant and animal species in existence are found there—they are decreasing rapidly, mostly at the hands of humans

POLAR REGIONS

The polar regions—the Arctic and Antarctica—cover the North and South Poles respectively, the northern- and southern-most tips of the earth.

The Arctic Ocean lies within the **Arctic Circle** and is surrounded almost entirely by land. Parts of this ocean are covered with ice all year long, and thousands of islands are scattered throughout its bitter cold waters. Despite the extremely cold temperatures, the Arctic does have a short summer during which it can get surprisingly warm. And unlike its more barren counterpart on the South Pole, the Arctic is actually home not only to icebergs and glaciers but also to rivers and lakes, mountains and forests, and even some flowers and vegetables.

The **Antarctic** is its own continent, with most of its lands covered in deep ice and snow at all times, supporting very few life forms. In wintertime, the ocean waters surrounding the continent freeze into huge, solid blocks of ice. As a whole, Antarctica is the coldest and windiest continent—the lowest temperature ever recorded was −128.6°F in 1983 at the Russian Vostok Station in Antarctica. It is also the driest, and despite the fact that more than 95 percent of the continent is covered in snow and ice, it actually gets relatively little new snow each year.

DESERTS

Deserts are dryer than any other places on the earth and receive very little rain or other precipitation. The terrain of deserts vary widely, from the freezing cold desert of Antarctica (the world's biggest) to dry, rocky mountainous regions to the miles of sand and dunes we generally picture when we think of deserts. Despite the barren landscapes, plenty of forms of life survive in the desert, including numerous varieties of flowers and plants that suddenly pop up in the rare event of rain, as well as cacti and other succulents that survive the dry weather by storing water within their body and roots. Deserts are found in Africa (including the Sahara), the Middle East, India, and Asia, as well as in North and South America.

MOUNTAIN REGIONS

Mountains are created by the slow, grinding movements of the earth's tectonic plates—when they collide, the earth's crust can fold or buckle, creating enormous mountain ranges all over the world. Their shape comes about in a variety of ways, including the way they were formed: volcanic activity that sometimes results from the melted rock of a sliding plate, the movement of glaciers that beautifully carve the land, erosion by time and weather, and other factors.

Mountain ranges can consist of many different kinds of trees and plants up to the timberline, the point at which the altitude no longer allows them to grow. The alpine regions, including the world's highest mountains such as the European Alps, the Himalayas, the Andes, and the Rockies, primarily support tundra plants, such as mosses and lichens, low shrubs and grasses, and some low-growing wildflowers.

OCEANS

Approximately 71 percent of our planet's surface is covered by oceans, large bodies of salt water that vary in temperature and average in depth at many thousands of feet. The major ocean divisions, from the largest to the smallest, are the Pacific Ocean, the Atlantic Ocean, the Indian Ocean, the Southern Ocean, and the Arctic Ocean. The currents of these oceans have a great influence on the earth's weather and biosphere. Oceans contain the largest number of life species, and new life continues to be discovered there as we increase our ability to explore the farthest depths.

Oceans contain many different habitats to support the rich and seemingly endless variety of species within them. These habitats include coral reefs, kelp forests, tidal zones, coastal areas, different surfaces of the ocean floor, and the open water itself, called the pelagic zone. The food chain within oceans is many layered, from the tiniest plankton to the largest blue whale, and its complexities are greatly threatened by the overfishing of some species by humans.

GRASSLANDS

Grasslands occur in areas where there is not enough rain for a forest to grow but too much rain for a desert to form. They are called many different things, depending on the location and the temperature of the region, which can vary greatly from hot summers with cold winters in some areas to year-round warmth in others. The colder grasslands include the prairies in North America, the pampas in South America, and the steppes in Europe and Asia. Grasslands with warmer temperatures include the savannahs in Africa and the rangelands in Australia. Grasslands are often used for grazing cattle, sheep, and other animals. Wheat, barley, oats, and rye can be found growing in some grasslands, whereas others support many low-growing flowering plants, trees, and bushes.

FORCES OF NATURE

Earthquakes happen when plates beneath the earth's surface shift, collide, or break, causing a sudden release of energy with ripples that can cause many potentially disastrous effects. These ripples, called seismic waves, can be measured by a seismograph. Multiple earthquakes happen across the world every single day, but most of them are too small to be noticed. Of the earthquakes we can actually feel, only a small percentage—approximately one every five years—results in extensive damage, including tsunamis, volcanic eruptions, landslides, and mass destruction of cities and human lives.

A **tornado** is a forceful, spinning column of air that bursts from an ominous-looking storm cloud, hits the ground violently (while simultaneously remaining connected to the base of the cloud), and begins moving forward, destroying virtually everything in its path. Tornadoes happen when winds from a thunderstorm or hurricane change pressure or direction and begin to spin more and more quickly. The average wind speed of tornadoes is between 40 and 110 miles per hour—although they have been recorded at speeds of more than 300 miles an hour—and they tend to travel at least several miles before they die out. (For more details, see TORNADOES: EARTH'S MOST VIOLENT STORMS on page 36.)

Hurricanes result when the winds from one or a collection of tropical storms pass over a large body of warm water, gather moisture and speed, and begin to swirl forcefully around a calmer, cooler center called the eye of the storm. To achieve hurricane status, the winds of a storm must reach 74 miles per hour (a Category 1 hurricane); severe hurricane winds have been recorded at speeds surpassing 160 miles per hour (a Category 5 hurricane). When these storms begin over the Pacific Ocean, they are called typhoons or cyclones instead of hurricanes. Once a hurricane moves from water to land, it can do a vast amount of damage. (For more details, see WHAT MAKES A STORM A HURRICANE? on page 37.)

A **blizzard** is a snowstorm with winds that must do the following: reach a minimum of 35 miles per hour, cause a severe lack of visibility with their blowing snow, and last for at least three hours. They also tend to have a windchill factor of at least −20°F. Blizzards happen when air that is cold enough, both in the clouds and on the ground, to form snow interacts with moisture and warmer air, creating strong winds and a huge amount of clouds and snow.

Floods are an overflow of too much water where it doesn't belong. They can be the result of a variety of different causes, including hurricanes, earthquakes, tsunamis, big rainstorms, and broken levees or dams.

A **drought** is an extended period of time during which an area of land endures a significant decrease in its water supply due primarily to a lack of rain and other precipitation. Droughts can last anywhere from a few weeks to several long years.

An **avalanche** is the fast and increasingly forceful flow of snow down the side of a mountain, with the potential to gather more and more snow and strength and destroy much in its path. Avalanches can be triggered by natural occurrences such as extra precipitation, falling rocks, or an earthquake, or by vibrations caused by human activities, such as skiing, snowmobiling, or the loud noises of construction work.

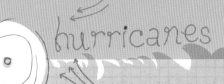
hurricanes

tornado

THE COLDEST WINTERS AND HOTTEST SUMMERS ON THE EARTH

Wildfires are fires that spread with great speed, grow to very large sizes, and cannot be controlled. They can often be caused by human error, such as campfires in the wilderness that are not fully extinguished, or human intention, like "slash and burn" clearing for land preparation. They are just as often the result of natural phenomenon, such as a strike of lightning during a heat wave or a volcanic eruption. While they can cause tremendous destruction of nature and human life, they also sometimes serve a beneficial purpose, helping forests continue natural cycles of reproduction and growth.

Volcanoes are essentially the mountains or hills that surround openings in the earth's surface, called craters, through which molten rock, gases, and debris can rise up. When the earth's enormous tectonic plates move and shift, pressure can build that causes magma (molten rock deep beneath the earth's surface) to rise and then erupt through the crater, becoming hot and often explosive lava as soon as it hits the air. Sudden and explosive eruptions can wreak tremendous havoc on the nature or the human population that surrounds them.

Auroras are breathtaking natural light shows in the skies above the North and South Poles. These enormous, shining rings of light happen when charged particles collide with the earth's magnetic field in the polar regions. They can measure more than 12,000 miles around and appear in many different forms, often with rays that look like huge, colorful curtains of light.

The South Pole in Antarctica has the earth's coldest wintertime temperature, with an average of about −72 °F. Fortunately no one lives there to endure this. As for inhabited locations, Siberia in Russia has the coldest winters. Verkhoyansk, in northeastern Siberia, has an annual average January temperature of −58°F and once recorded a low of −90°F.

On the other end of the spectrum, the hottest summers on the planet occur in such notorious hot spots such as Death Valley, California; parts of the Sahara Desert in Mali and Algeria; and in the delta of the Tigris and Euphrates rivers, on the border of Iraq and Iran. All endure incredibly hot summers, with high temperatures soaring well into the 110s and 120s on a regular basis.

DEATH VALLEY

ANTARCTICA

TORNADOES: EARTH'S MOST VIOLENT STORMS

Tornadoes are the most violent storms on the earth. Winds spiraling into them usually exceed 100 miles per hour and can reach speeds of 300 miles per hour. In the United States, an average of 1,000 tornadoes spin up beneath thunderstorms each year, and these typically kill about 60 people per year.

Tornadoes and the threat of tornadoes are a key part of the U.S. spring weather because spring brings favorable tornado conditions. But tornadoes can occur any time of the year, during the day and at night.

The National Weather Service defines a tornado as "a violently rotating column of air in contact with the ground and pendant from a thunderstorm." In other words, a thunderstorm is the first step in the creation of a tornado. Then, if other conditions are right, the thunderstorm might spin out one or more tornadoes.

The three key conditions required for thunderstorms to form are these:

- Moisture in the lower to midlevels of the atmosphere.
- Unstable air. That is, air that will continue rising once it begins rising from near the ground.
- A lifting force. Something is needed to cause the air to begin rising. The most common lifting force is the heating of air near the ground. As the air warms, it

becomes lighter and begins rising. Advancing masses of cool air close to the ground which forces warm air upward, also trigger thunderstorms.

When all the conditions are present, humid air will rise high into the sky and cool and condense into towering clouds, forming thunderstorms. This air rising into a thunderstorm is called an updraft. Tornadoes form within a thunderstorm's updraft.

The strongest tornadoes are often near the edge of the updraft, not far from where air is descending in a downdraft caused by the thunderstorms with falling rain or hail. This is why a burst of heavy rain or hail sometimes announces a tornado's arrival.

Tornadoes are commonly associated with the nation's heartland—in a ten-state area stretching from Texas to Nebraska that also includes Colorado, Iowa, Illinois, Indiana, Missouri, and Arkansas, known as Tornado Alley. But, they are not limited to this region. Tornadoes have occurred in all fifty states and are, in fact, more common in Florida than they are in Oklahoma, although tornadoes in Florida are generally much weaker.

Most weak tornadoes last ten minutes or less, traveling short distances. Violent tornadoes have been known to last for hours, and a few have traveled more than 100 miles.

WHAT MAKES A STORM A HURRICANE?

Hurricanes and other cyclones that form in the tropics during summer and fall are very different from the extratropical storms that often form during winter, even though both can produce very strong winds and flooding rain.

The seven main characteristics that define a hurricane, and all tropical cyclones, are these:

- Hurricanes have no fronts.
- Hurricane winds weaken with altitude.
- The centers of hurricanes are warmer than their surroundings.
- Hurricanes and tropical systems form under weak high-altitude winds.
- Air sinks at the center of a hurricane.
- Hurricanes' main energy source is the latent heat of condensation.
- Hurricanes weaken rapidly over land.

Tropical systems are classified into four categories according to the degree of organization and maximum sustained wind speed.

Tropical disturbance, tropical wave: Unorganized mass of thunderstorms; very little, if any, organized wind circulation.

Tropical depression: Has evidence of closed wind circulation around a center with sustained winds from 20 to 34 knots (23–39 mph).

Tropical storm: Maximum sustained winds are from 35 to 64 knots (40–74 mph). The storm is named once it reaches tropical storm strength.

Hurricane or typhoon: Maximum sustained winds exceed 64 knots (74 mph).

Hurricanes are classified into different categories according to the Saffir Simpson scale. As they move inland, hurricanes can also spawn severe weather, such as tornadoes.

UNDERSTANDING CLIMATE CHANGE

UNDERSTANDING CLIMATE CHANGE

Global warming is shorthand for climate change, and the term is correct if you realize that it's referring to the average temperature of the earth over years and decades, not to the temperatures at particular times and places.

Climate change is a more descriptive term because it involves much more than warming, although the changes first begin with the globe's average warming. This average warming can cause changes in patterns of rainfall. It can lead to more snow piling up in places such as Antarctica and Greenland, and it can even cause some parts of the earth to grow colder.

Scientists have managed to figure out a general, fairly detailed picture of the earth's climate going back more than 100,000 years, before the beginning of the last ice age. This history shows that temperatures of different parts of the earth, and even the earth's average temperature, have swung widely in the past, into and out of ice ages long before humans could have affected the climate.

Still, climate scientists say the evidence is strong that humans are responsible for much of the warming since early in the twentieth century.

There's no doubt that the amount of carbon dioxide in the air—a greenhouse gas—has increased. This increase in a greenhouse gas is bound to "force" the climate in one direction or another, with a general warming being one of the effects.

MAKE IT RIGHT FOUNDATION

BRAD PITT

BRAD PITT'S MAKE IT RIGHT FOUNDATION

When Brad Pitt first laid eyes on the devastation Hurricane Katrina wrought on the Lower Ninth Ward of New Orleans in 2005, he was shocked at both the extent of the damage and the absence of a clear plan to address it. Many seemed to be giving up hope of ever saving this important piece of New Orleans and the United States, so rich with history and cultural diversity. So this movie star with a strong interest in architecture and advocacy began to really listen to the concerns of those who lived—or used to live—in the Ninth Ward and vowed to rebuild the decimated neighborhood, making it stronger and more environmentally sound than it was before, while preserving the same warm community feel and nourishing the same soul that had lived there for so long.

In the years since Make It Right began, Pitt has worked and consulted with experts around the world, but he has also spent a great deal of time listening to the residents themselves and working with local community leaders to create top-quality, sustainable, and affordable design that still preserves the community's culture and spirit.

For more information and the latest updates, see the Web site at makeitrightnola.org.

USA TODAY Snapshots®

Environmentally friendly choices

Nearly 40% of adults say recycling is the most beneficial thing they can do for the environment. How other "green" practices rate:

28%
Buying renewable energy

19%
Using greener transportation

7%
Selecting minimal or reduced packaging

Source: Green Seal and EnviroMedia Social Marketing survey of 1,000 adults by Opinion Research Corp. Margin of error ±3.2 percentage points.

By Michelle Healy and Alejandro Gonzalez, USA TODAY

HAVE YOU HEARD?

COMPOSTING is just like recycling your food! Yuck! Actually, this really cool process breaks down food waste (such as banana peels), yard waste (such as grass clippings), or other compostable material (such as paper coffee cups) and turns it into a nutrient-rich soil that helps your garden grow. There is a wide range of composting techniques, including outdoor bins that use heat from the sun to process the material and indoor vermicomposters that use tiny worms to do the work. More and more cities are starting to use composting as an alternative to landfills. The food and yard waste is collected from your home, processed in big industrial composters, and sold as high-quality soil in garden stores.

JONAS BROTHERS

DISNEY'S STARS ASK KIDS TO GO GREEN

Disney favorites Miley Cyrus, Demi Lovato, Selena Gomez, and the Jonas Brothers are encouraging kids to help the planet. Disney has just announced that these stars are among twenty-nine participating in Project Green, helping to get the word out on the Disney Channel and Radio Disney to get kids involved by changing small daily actions to have a big environmental impact. Kids can join online at disney.com and vote on how Disney distributes $1 million to environmental causes.

EARTH HOUR: Turning Lights Off To Take Action!

EARTH HOUR: TURNING LIGHTS OFF TO TAKE ACTION!

World Wildlife Fund's Earth Hour is an inspiring global event created to symbolize what a positive impact every one of us can have on climate change when we work together. On March 28 each year, millions of people from cities across the world work together to express their concern about climate change and their commitment to make a difference with one simple action: turning off their lights for one hour. Earth Hour began in 2007 in Sydney, Australia. The following year Earth Hour was embraced by more than 400 cities and 50 million people around the world, as well as thousands more businesses and vital landmarks from across the globe, including Sydney's Opera House, Rome's Colosseum, London's City Hall, New York's Empire State Building, San Francisco's Golden Gate Bridge, the Google homepage, and many more.

In the words of Carter S. Roberts, the president and CEO of the World Wildlife Fund: "This is the perfect opportunity for individuals, governments, schools, businesses, and communities around the world to unite for a common purpose, in response to a global issue that affects us all."

For more information and current updates, see the Web site worldwildlife.org.

Popular Culture

bono

CELEBRITIES MAKING A DIFFERENCE

George Clooney

For years, acclaimed actor and beloved idol George Clooney has been dedicated to the cause of improving the dangerous lives of refugees from the war-torn Darfur region of the Sudan. It is a painful and uphill battle to get the support and change these people need, but as a UN Messenger of Peace and cofounder of the organization Not On Our Watch (notonourwatchproject.org), Clooney shows no signs of backing down.

Bono

U2's lead singer and international rock star, Bono, is the cofounder of One (one.org), a nonpartisan, grassroots campaign and advocacy organization dedicated to the fight against poverty and preventable disease, particularly the spread of AIDS in Africa. The organization is backed by more than two million people and works closely with policy experts, activists, and world leaders to bring about the most effective and lasting changes.

★ ★ ★ ★ ★ ★

george

Angelina Jolie

Angelina Jolie, named the most powerful celebrity in the world by *Forbes* magazine in 2009, is far more than an Academy Award–winning movie star—she is also a mother, a business woman, and a tireless humanitarian. In addition to giving millions of dollars to charities each year, Jolie is a goodwill ambassador for the UN Refugee Agency for her work on behalf of refugees in Cambodia, Jordan, and other countries, and in 2005, she received a Global Humanitarian Action Award for her work as an activist for refugee rights. She is also the founder of the Maddox Jolie-Pitt Foundation, which works to support conservation and development efforts in Cambodia.

Shakira

Shakira, a popular singer and celebrity from Colombia who has become one of the top-selling female vocalists in the world, is also a powerful advocate for early-childhood development and education, particularly in Latin America. Shakira's charitable endeavors began when she was eighteen, and eventually she became one of the founders of *Fundación América Latina en Acción Solidaria*, or ALAS ("wings" in Spanish), a group of Ibero-American singers using their fame and connections to further the cause of early-childhood development.

Leonardo DiCaprio

The acclaimed actor and heartthrob Leonardo DiCaprio has also been a passionate environmental advocate for many years. In 1998, he founded the Leonardo DiCaprio Foundation (leonardodicaprio.org) to promote the awareness and advancement of many environmental issues, particularly the climate crisis. In 2001, the foundation received the prestigious Martin Litton Environmental Warrior Award from Environment Now; it has since joined with the California Community Foundation and is now called The Leonardo DiCaprio Fund at CCF. His feature length documentary, *The 11th Hour*, focuses on global warming, the sustainability movement, and other ecological concerns.

MOVIES

SEAN PENN

TOP TEN GROSSING U.S. MOVIES OF ALL TIME *

1. *Titanic* (1997)
2. *The Dark Knight* (2008)
3. *Star Wars* (1977)
4. *Shrek 2* (2004)
5. *E.T.: The Extra-Terrestrial* (1982)
6. *Star Wars: Episode I—The Phantom Menace* (1999)
7. *Pirates of the Caribbean: Dead Man's Chest* (2006)
8. *Spider-Man* (2002)
9. *Transformers: Revenge of the Fallen* (2009)
10. *Star Wars: Episode III—Revenge of the Sith* (2005)

*As of November 30, 2009

DANNY BOYLE

THE OSCARS—HIGHLIGHTS (2009)

Picture: *Slumdog Millionaire*

Actor in a Leading Role: Sean Penn, *Milk*

Actress in a Leading Role: Kate Winslet, *The Reader*

Actor in a Supporting Role: Heath Ledger, *The Dark Knight*

Actress in a Supporting Role: Penelope Cruz, *Vicky Christina Barcelona*

Directing: Danny Boyle, *Slumdog Millionaire*

Music (Song): *Slumdog Millionaire*

Documentary Feature: *Man on Wire*

Animated Feature Film: *Wall-E*

Writing (Adapted Screenplay): *Slumdog Millionaire*

Writing (Original Screenplay): *Milk*

TOP TEN GROSSING U.S. MOVIES OF ALL TIME—ADJUSTED FOR INFLATION *

1. *Gone with the Wind* (1939)
2. *Star Wars* (1977)
3. *The Sound of Music* (1965)
4. *E.T.: The Extra-Terrestrial* (1982)
5. *The Ten Commandments* (1956)
6. *Titanic* (1997)
7. *Jaws* (1975)
8. *Doctor Zhivago* (1965)
9. *The Exorcist* (1973)
10. *Snow White and the Seven Dwarfs* (1937)

*As of November 30, 2009

OSCAR

TEEN CHOICE AWARDS— MOVIE HIGHLIGHTS (2009)

Actor, Action Adventure: Hugh Jackman, *X-Men Origins: Wolverine*

Actor, Comedy: Zac Efron, *17 Again*

Actor, Drama: Robert Pattinson, *Twilight*

Actor, Music/Dance: Zac Efron, *High School Musical 3: Senior Year*

Actress, Action Adventure: Jordana Brewster, *Fast & Furious*

Actress, Comedy: Anne Hathaway, *Bride Wars*

Actress, Drama: Kristen Stewart, *Twilight*

Actress, Music/Dance: Miley Cyrus, *Hannah Montana: The Movie*

Movie, Action Adventure: *X-Men Origins: Wolverine*

Movie, Drama: *Twilight*

Movie, Horror/Thriller: *Friday the 13th*

Movie, Liplock: Kristen Stewart and Robert Pattinson, *Twilight*

Movie, Music/Dance: *High School Musical 3: Senior Year*

Movie, Romance: *Twilight*

Movie, Rumble: Robert Pattinson vs. Cam Gigandet, *Twilight*

Movie, Comedy: *Night at the Museum: Battle of the Smithsonian*

TOP TEN GROSSING MOVIES (2009) *

1. *Transformers: Revenge of the Fallen*
2. *Harry Potter and the Half-Blood Prince*
3. *Up*
4. *The Hangover*
5. *Star Trek*
6. *Twilight Saga: New Moon*
7. *Monsters vs. Aliens*
8. *Ice Age: Dawn of the Dinosaurs*
9. *X-Men Origins: Wolverine*
10. *Night at the Museum: Battle of the Smithsonian*

*As of November 30, 2009

X-MEN: WOLVERINE

STAR TREK

UP

HARRY POTTER AND THE DEATHLY HALLOWS

This last installment of the beloved Harry Potter series will no doubt break records! The sixth film in the series, *Harry Potter and the Half-Blood Prince*, ranks as the number one film of 2009 on the worldwide charts.

DANIEL RADCLIFFE

NIGHT AT THE MUSEUM

ROBERT PATTINSON AND KRISTIN STEWART

MILEY CYRUS: *HANNAH MONTANA AND BEYOND*

An overnight star at twelve thanks to the Disney Channel's *Hannah Montana* series, Miley Cyrus aka Miley Stewart aka Hannah Montana, has sold more than 7 million albums, launched a popular WalMart clothing line, and made a concert film that raked in $70 million.

But wait, there's more. In the soundtrack from *Hannah Montana: The Movie*, Cyrus unleashed a power-ballad single ("The Climb") and takes a line-dancing page from dad Billy Ray's book (the rap 'n' twang ditty "Hoedown Throwdown"). She also plugged songs by her father, Taylor Swift, and country pals Rascal Flatts, all while telling the tale of an ingenue replanted in the southern soil that kept her rooted through Hollywood storms.

When asked about television, concerts, and boyfriends, Cyrus dutifully pumps out answers that are honest but rote. But compliment her acting, and she suddenly halts her teen habits—checking her PDA, fiddling with her nails—and beams.

"People don't think Disney stars are in it for the art, but I love acting," says Cyrus, comfy in jeans, a gray hooded sweatshirt, high-heeled boots and coaster-size hoop earrings. "I was constantly stretching in this movie, and though I wouldn't change anything I did in it, I'm really looking forward to the next one."

Cyrus's appeal now, Tarnoff says, is an "every teen" quality that combines normalcy with a hint of brilliance. "She's really pretty without being *impossibly* pretty. She's attainably awesome."

MILEY CYRUS: Hannah Montana and Beyond

AVATAR

This science fiction film, written and directed by **James Cameron**, is as groundbreaking in its technology and scope as *Star Wars* was when it first came out in 1977. Richard Corliss from *TIME* magazine said: "For years to come, it will define what movies can achieve." With its stereoscopic filmmaking, breathtaking 3D and IMAX 3D viewing, and epic futuristic storyline, *Avatar* captured the world's imagination at the end of 2009 and quickly became one of the highest grossing movies of all time.

TAYLOR SWIFT

Taylor Swift is the spunky and talented country-and-pop singer-songwriter and guitarist whom *Billboard* magazine named 2009 Artist of the Year at age twentieth—and with good reason. After combined sales of her first two albums (*Taylor Swift* and *Fearless*) made her the best-selling musician of 2008 in the United States, Swift went on to dazzle audiences and win multiple awards throughout 2009, including MTV Music Awards Best Female Video, Academy of Country Music's "Crystal Milestone Award," Country Music Awards Entertainer of the Year, and the American Music Awards Artist of the Year. With more than 24.3 million digital tracks sold by January 2010, Swift also became the top-selling digital artist in music history.

MUSIC

TOP-SELLING ALBUMS 2009

1. *Fearless*, Taylor Swift (3.2 million)
2. *I Dreamed a Dream*, Susan Boyle (3.1 million)
3. *Number Ones*, Michael Jackson (2.4 million)
4. *The Fame*, Lady Gaga (2.2 million)
5. *My Christmas*, Andrea Bocelli (2.2 million)
6. *Hannah Montana: The Movie*, Soundtrack (1.8 million)
7. *The E.N.D. (Energy Never Dies)*, the Black Eyed Peas (1.8 million)
8. *Relapse*, Eminem (1.7 million)
9. *The Blueprint 3*, Jay-Z (1.5 million)
10. *Only by the Night*, Kings of Leon (1.4 million)

TEEN CHOICE AWARDS—MUSIC HIGHLIGHTS (2009)

Album, Female Artist: *Fearless*, Taylor Swift

Album, Group: *Lines, Vines and Trying Times*, Jonas Brothers

Album, Male Artist: *We Sing, We Dance, We Steal Things*, Jason Mraz

Artist, Female: Taylor Swift

Artist, Male: Jason Mraz

Artist, Breakout: David Archuleta

Single: "The Climb," Miley Cyrus

Love Song: "Crush," David Archuleta

R&B Artist: Beyoncé

R&B Track: "Single Ladies (Put a Ring on It)," Beyoncé

Rap Artist: Kanye West

Rap/Hip-Hop Track: "Boom Boom Pow," Black Eyed Peas

Rock Group: Paramore

Rock Track: "Decode," Paramore

Soundtrack: *Twilight*

Tour: David Archuleta/Demi Lovato

Beyoncé

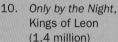

★ HAVE YOU HEARD? ★

Susan Boyle is an unassuming, everyday-looking Scottish woman who dazzled the world with a spectacular singing voice—that no one expected during her audition for the reality show *Britain's Got Talent.* Within days of airing, video of the show-stopping performance that caught everyone by surprise was seen on YouTube more than 100 million times, and Boyle went on to record the album *I Dreamed a Dream*, which became the second highest grossing album of 2009.

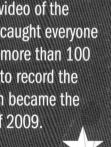

TAYLOR SWIFT

BLACK EYED PEAS

2009: MTV VIDEO MUSIC AWARDS

Video of the Year: Beyoncé, *Single Ladies (Put a Ring on It)*

Best Male Video: T.I. featuring Rihanna, *Live Your Life*

Best Female Video: Taylor Swift, *You Belong with Me*

Best Hip-Hop Video: Eminem, *We Made You*

Best Pop Video: Britney Spears, *Womanizer*

Best Rock Video: Green Day, *21 Guns*

Breakthrough Video: Matt and Kim, *Lessons Learned*

Best New Artist: Lady Gaga, *Poker Face*

★ HAVE YOU ★ HEARD?

In the summer of 2009, Jason Mraz's happy love song "I'm Yours" made history as the longest running song in the history of the *Billboard* Hot 100 chart.

COLDPLAY

SOME HOT MUSIC ARTISTS

Beyoncé

Black Eyed Peas

Carrie Underwood

Coldplay

Jason Mraz

Jonas Brothers

Katy Perry

Kelly Clarkson

Taylor Swift

KATY PERRY

TAYLOR SWIFT

LADY GAGA

ALEC BALDWIN

TELEVISION

PRIME-TIME EMMY AWARDS—HIGHLIGHTS

Outstanding Comedy Series:
30 Rock

Oustanding Drama Series:
Mad Men

Outstanding Made-for-Television Movie: *Grey Gardens*

Outstanding Miniseries: *Little Dorrit*

Outstanding Reality-Competition Program:
The Amazing Race

Outstanding Variety, Music, or Comedy Series:
The Daily Show with Jon Stewart

Outstanding Lead Actor in a Comedy Series:
Alec Baldwin, *30 Rock*

Outstanding Lead Actress in a Comedy Series:
Toni Collette, *United States of Tara*

Outstanding Supporting Actor in a Comedy Series: Jon Cryer, *Two and a Half Men*

Outstanding Supporting Actress in a Comedy Series: Kristin Chenoweth, *Pushing Daisies*

Outstanding Lead Actor in a Drama Series: Bryan Cranston, *Breaking Bad*

Outstanding Lead Actress in a Drama Series: Glenn Close, *Damages*

Outstanding Supporting Actor in a Drama Series: Michael Emerson, *Lost*

Outstanding Supporting Actress in a Drama Series: Cherry Jones, *24*

Outstanding Lead Actor in a Miniseries or a Movie: Brendan Gleeson, *In the Storm*

Outstanding Lead Actress in a Miniseries or a Movie: Jessica Lange, *Grey Gardens*

Outstanding Host for a Reality or Reality-Competition Program: Jeff Probst, *Survivor*

TOP TEN TV SHOWS (2009)

1. *American Idol* (Wednesday)
2. *American Idol* (Tuesday)
3. *Dancing with the Stars*
4. *NBC Sunday Night Football*
5. *Dancing with the Stars* (Results Show)
6. *NCIS: Los Angeles*
7. *NCIS*
8. *NFL Regular Season*
9. *Sunday Night NFL Pre-kick*
10. *The Good Wife*

JUSTIN TIMBERLAKE   30 ROCK

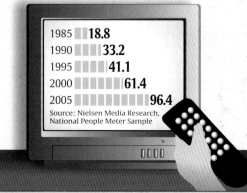

USA TODAY Snapshots®

At home with more TV channels

The number of television channels that the average U.S. home receives rose to 104.2 in 2006. How that number has grown:

Year	Channels
1985	18.8
1990	33.2
1995	41.1
2000	61.4
2005	96.4

Source: Nielsen Media Research, National People Meter Sample

By Cindy Clark and Alejandro Gonzalez, USA TODAY

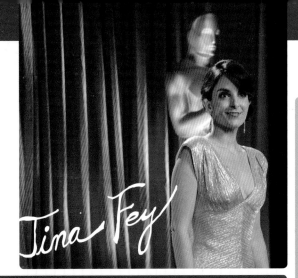

Tina Fey

TINA FEY

Tina Fey is a multiple-award-winning actress, writer, comedienne, and producer. After years doing improv with the Second City in Chicago, Tina Fey joined the writing staff of *Saturday Night Live* in 1997. Two years later, she became the first female head writer in *SNL* history and began performing on the show as well, co-anchoring "Weekend Update" with Jimmy Fallon and then with Amy Poehler. In 2004, she wrote and acted in the popular movie *Mean Girls*, and left *SNL* in 2006 to write, produce, and star in NBC's hit sitcom *30 Rock*. She starred with Poehler in the feature comedy *Baby Mama* in 2008 and also returned to *SNL* that year for some hilarious guest spots portraying vice presidential nominee Sarah Palin.

iCARLY

Tons of teens love this hit cable show, and so do many of their parents, making it a great show the whole family can watch together. Miranda Cosgrove plays Carly, a smart and spunky girl who produces her own Internet series. Whitney Matheson from *USA Today* said: "I expected cheesy jokes, but the writing is actually smarter than it has to be. I love that the main character is smart, ambitious, and has something better to do with her time than talk about boys and hair."

NATHAN KRESS, MIRANDA COSGROVE, AND JENNETTE MCCURDY

TEEN CHOICE AWARDS— TV HIGHLIGHTS (2009)

Actor, Action Adventure: Tom Welling, *Smallville*

Actor, Comedy: Jonas Brothers, *Jonas*

Actor, Drama: Chace Crawford, *Gossip Girl*

Actress, Action Adventure: Hayden Panettiere, *Heroes*

Actress, Comedy: Miley Cyrus, *Hannah Montana*

Actress, Drama: Leighton Meester, *Gossip Girl*

Breakout Star, Female: Demi Lovato, *Sonny with a Chance*

Breakout Star, Male: Frankie Jonas, *Jonas*

Reality/Variety Star, Female: Lauren Conrad, *The Hills*

Reality/Variety Star, Male: Adam Lambert, *American Idol*

Personality: Ryan Seacrest, *American Idol*, *E! News*

Sidekick: Emily Osment, *Hannah Montana*

Villain: Ed Westwick, *Gossip Girl*

Show, Action Adventure: *Heroes*

Show, Animated: *SpongeBob SquarePants*

Show, Breakout Show: *Jonas*

Show, Comedy: *Hannah Montana*

Show, Drama: *Gossip Girl*

Show, Late Night: *Chelsea Lately*

Show, Reality: *The Hills*

Show, Reality Competition: *American Idol*

Jonas Brothers

JONAS BROTHERS

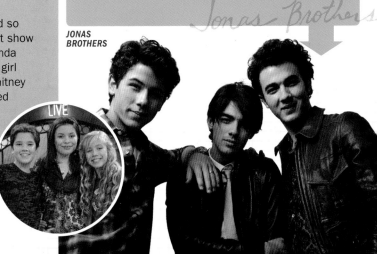

BOOKS | THE WIMPY KID GETS KIDS READING

GREG HEFFLEY

Greg Heffley, aka The Wimpy Kid, is a wisecracking, self-centered middle schooler whose life is filled with suburban misadventures. He has an oversized head, a prominent nose, and three strands of hair. No one knows exactly how old he is or where he lives, not even his not-so-wimpy creator, Jeff Kinney.

Greg is a cartoon character and the star of Kinney's books, the *Diary of a Wimpy Kid* series. Millions of copies of these books have sold in the United States alone, and they have been translated into at least twenty-eight other languages.

The books are designed to look as if written and illustrated by Greg, the middle schooler. As an author, Kinney, who has kept his day job designing online games, is most popular among fifth-grade boys. But he also appeals to girls, parents, librarians, and teachers. Grateful grown-ups say his series has taken the word *reluctant* out of *reluctant readers*, many of whom who are suddenly finding themselves devouring these books in a matter of days.

"I didn't start out by trying to turn nonreaders into readers," Kinney says. "It was sort of a lark. I'm not a strong writer of narrative fiction, but I can string jokes together. And I'm happy the books have become a gateway to legitimate reading."

Greg's diary entries complain about bullies when he's not bullying others. He works harder on avoiding chores and homework than on doing them. He's sandwiched between older and younger brothers who cause all the problems (as he sees it). He has an enthusiastic mom he's easily embarrassed by and a dad who's frustrated Greg isn't more of an athlete.

As Greg puts it, "I tried to explain how with video games, you can play sports like football and soccer, and you don't even get all hot and sweaty. But as usual, Dad didn't see my logic."

Greg "isn't a character to be emulated," Kinney says. "But I think kids get that. They're more sophisticated than we think. They laugh at Bart Simpson, but they know you're not supposed to be like Bart Simpson."

For the cover of the first book, its main color—burnt red—was chosen to match the cover of J. D. Salinger's *The Catcher in the Rye*, which also has a discontented narrator, if older and more jaded. "Greg is like Holden Caulfield," Kinney's editor says. "What he doesn't like in others he's guilty of himself. Kids recognize that. And when you identify with something, you can rise above it." The overriding joke, Kinney says, is that "Greg is a deeply flawed protagonist . . . Kids get that Greg isn't perfect, and I think that's why they like him."

Kinney first heard the term *reluctant reader* in letters from parents and teachers: "I thought, 'What a curious turn of phrase.'" He has since learned "the reluctant-reader issue is huge, especially among boys. Reluctant readers are just kids who have so many entertainment options—the Internet, television, video games—they don't see the value of reading."

Recognizing the growing competition, schools and libraries are increasingly embracing comic books and graphic novels. (Kinney calls his "novels in cartoons.") Pat Scales, a middle-school librarian for twenty-eight years and president of the Association for Library Service to Children, says Kinney's series is "terrific at dealing with the everyday life of middle schoolers in a funny way. Kids that age need humor in their lives."

"What he doesn't like in others he's guilty of himself."

BOOKS

TOP TEN BEST BOOKS FOR YOUNG ADULTS (2009)

It's Complicated: The American Teenager by Robin Bowman

Waiting for Normal by Leslie Connor

Mexican WhiteBoy by Matt de la Pena

Bog Child by Siobhan Dowd

The Hunger Games by Suzanne Collins

Ten Cents a Dance by Christine Fletcher

Baby by Joseph Monninger

Nation by Terry Pratchett

Skim by Mariko Tamaki and Jillian Tamaki

The Brothers Torres by Coert Voorhees

TWILIGHT
(THE MOVIE)

INTERNET

FRED!: YOUTUBE AND INTERNET SENSATION

Lucas Cruikshank is a teenager from Columbus, Nebraska, whose *Fred!* videos on YouTube are a huge sensation, garnering him a guest spot on Nickelodeon's hot show *iCarly*, as well as a Teen Choice Award for Web Star in 2009. The *Fred Channel* on YouTube has well over one million subscribers.

 Lucas created the character Fred Figglehorn himself: he is a six-year-old who talks a fast blue streak in a high, squeaky voice. Fred has a recovering alcoholic mother and a problem temper. All other characters, including a girl he has a crush on in his kindergarten class and a boy who is his mortal enemy, are also played by Lucas.

Lucas first post as Fred!—called "Fred on Halloween" and posted when he was fourteen years old—was basically a joke, parodying people on YouTube who post blogs about the details of their lives, assuming that people will be interested. Lucas can see how some people find Fred! irritating, but also feels that he really has heart. At least some of the more than 380 million cumulative viewers who have viewed his videos must agree.

★ HAVE YOU HEARD? ★

THE *TWILIGHT* PHENOMENON

This four-book saga tells the story of what happens when girl meets vampire. When Bella moves to dreary Forks, Washington, and enrolls in high school, she meets a mysterious and dreamy boy in her class named Edward Cullen. Bella and Edward are drawn to each other, but they've got one pretty big problem: he's a vampire, who survives by drinking blood. In this series, author Stephenie Meyer introduces us to Edward's complicated and enchanting family of vampires who are determined to overcome their violent instincts and be moral creatures who blend into society without hurting anyone. The books involve romance, fantasy, and lots of excitement as Bella and Edward fall madly in love, and Edward vows to protect Bella from the danger that seems to follow her everywhere—including himself.

twilight

TWITTER FOUNDERS:
JACK DORSEY,
BIZ STONE,
EVAN WILLIAMS

tweet !

TWITTER

Twitter is a Web site (twitter.com) with a very simple idea: answer the question, what's happening? in 140 characters or less (called a tweet) whenever you feel like it, and read what other people are doing by "following" them, which is kind of like subscribing to their tweets. Twitter's popularity has skyrocketed, and now it's considered part of the social-media boom along with sites like Facebook. As more and more people start tweeting, you can find all sorts of interesting people to follow, from your friends to celebrities, comedians, news outlets, politicians, businesses, and more. Whether you like to tweet a lot or you'd rather just read what's out there, Twitter is a great way to learn and share information and stay connected with what's happening in your community and around the world.

★ ★ ★ ★ ★ ★

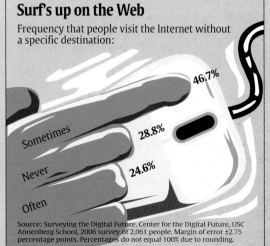

USA TODAY Snapshots®

Surf's up on the Web

Frequency that people visit the Internet without a specific destination:

46.7%

Sometimes 28.8%

Never 24.6%

Often

Source: Surveying the Digital Future, Center for the Digital Future, USC Annenberg School, 2006 survey of 2,061 people. Margin of error ±2.75 percentage points. Percentages do not equal 100% due to rounding.

By Cindy Clark and Robert W. Ahrens, USA TODAY

tweet !

Science & Technology

SCIENCE DEFINED

The term *science* (derived from the Latin root *scientia*, which means "knowledge") refers both to a system of obtaining knowledge through experimentation and observation and to the established field of shared knowledge that has resulted from this system. The information that science primarily seeks to uncover concerns all aspects of ourselves and the world around us, in the never-ending quest for human knowledge that is backed up by disciplined observation of reliable data. This investigatory system of observation and research is called the scientific method.

The many different types of science are often classified within several fields. The field of **natural sciences** involves the study of the natural world and all of its phenomena, and they include the major branches of physical sciences, earth sciences, environmental sciences, and life sciences. The field of **social sciences** focuses on the behavior and interactions of humans. The field of **formal sciences** involves the formulation and analysis of theories and laws that have contributed greatly to the progress of both the natural and physical sciences. Each general field of science contains many specific types of science within it, some of which are described here.

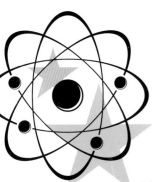

FIELDS OF SCIENCE

Formal Sciences
Computer science: theories of what and how information can be automated

Logic: inference and reasoning

Mathematics: quantifiable data, relationships, conjectures, and patterns

Statistics: collection, interpretation, and presentation of data

Social Sciences
Anthropology: human cultures and physical traits throughout time

Economics: production and distribution of goods and services

Political science: theory and practice of political systems and governmental institutions

Psychology: individual mental processes and behavior of humans and animals

Sociology: human activity and behavior in groups

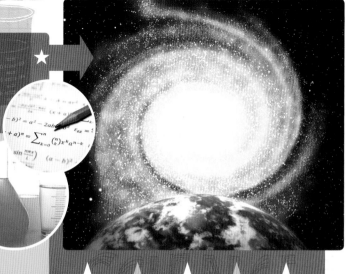

Natural Sciences

There are four fields of natural science: Physical Sciences, Earth Sciences, Environmental Sciences, and Life Sciences.

PHYSICAL SCIENCES

Astronomy: celestial objects (stars, planets, comets) and any occurrence outside of the earth's atmosphere

Chemistry: structure, properties, and behavior of matter

Physics: matter and how it moves, through energy and force

EARTH SCIENCES

Climatology: weather conditions over time

Geography: features of the earth's terrain

Geology: the earth's inner materials

Hydrology: water throughout the earth

Meteorology: atmosphere and weather

Oceanography: oceans, currents, tides, and habitats

Paleontology: prehistoric life of plants and animals

Seismology: earthquakes

Topography: surface shape of the earth

Volcanology: volcanoes

ENVIRONMENTAL SCIENCES

Ecology: interactions between organisms and their environment

Environmental chemistry: natural chemical occurrences

Toxicology: negative effects of chemicals on living organisms

LIFE SCIENCES

Anatomy: structure of living things

Biochemistry: chemical processes in living organisms

Botany: plant life

Genetics: heredity and variety in living organisms

Microbiology: microscopic organisms

Molecular biology: interactions within cells

Physiology: physical and biochemical processes of living organisms

Zoology: behavior and development of animals

FAMOUS SCIENTISTS THROUGHOUT HISTORY

Nicolaus Copernicus (1473–1543): a Prussian mathematician, astronomer, and well-rounded Renaissance man, is most revered for his landmark theory (now a proven fact) that the earth is neither flat nor the center of the universe, but rather that it revolves around the sun, as well as rotates on its own axis. This notion of the sun, rather than the earth, being at the center of the universe was a seminal moment in history that began the scientific revolution.

Charles Darwin (1809–82): an English naturalist most famous for his revolutionary theory of evolution by a process he termed *natural selection*. This theory—that all living creatures have evolved over time from a common set of ancestors, gradually changing to best survive in their surroundings—is to this day a vital foundation of all life sciences.

Galileo Galilei (1564–1642): an Italian astronomer and philosopher whose work—including vital improvements to the telescope and the resulting astronomical discoveries, as well as his passionate support of Copernicanism (see above)—has led many to refer to him as the father of modern science.

Louis Pasteur (1822–95): a French chemist whose work set the stage for all future studies in microbiology and immunology. His groundbreaking discoveries regarding the causes and preventions of sickness and disease led to the first human vaccines and the process known as *pasteurization*—which made milk and wine, and eventually many other foods and beverages, far safer to consume—among other important findings.

Johannes Kepler (1571–1630): a German mathematician and astronomer most remembered for his discovery that the earth and other planets orbit around the sun, and his subsequent and foundational laws of planetary motion. He also did important optical work on the telescope and helped to validate the discoveries of fellow astronomer Galileo Galilei.

Isaac Newton (1642–1727): an English mathematician and astronomer who discovered and explained gravitational force and the three laws of motion. He, along with German scientist Gottfried von Leibniz, is also credited with inventing calculus.

Sigmund Freud (1856–1939): an Austrian neurologist and psychologist who is considered the founding father of psychoanalysis. His provocative theories regarding sexuality, repression, and the nature of the unconscious mind continue to divide people to this day, but despite the controversy his work engenders, he remains one of the most influential thinkers of the twentieth century.

Antoine-Laurent Lavoisier (1743–94): a French nobleman and scientist whom many call the father of modern chemistry is most known for his discovery and naming of oxygen and hydrogen, his findings regarding the vital role oxygen plays in combustion, and for writing the first comprehensive list of elements.

Albert Einstein (1879–1955): a German American physicist best known for his groundbreaking *theory of relativity*, which explores the relationships between time, distance, energy, and matter, and the formula $E=mc^2$. He won the Nobel Prize in Physics in 1921 and also spent his time as a pacifist and social activist concerned that his work was to be used for military purposes (which it sadly was).

Neils Bohr (1885–1962): a Danish physicist whose work on the structure of atoms won him the Nobel Prize in Physics in 1922 and eventually led to the invention of quantum mechanics.

Jane Goodall (1934–): an English anthropologist and primatologist whose lifelong work with chimpanzees, especially regarding their social and familial interactions, has had powerful effects on our scientific studies of the evolution and definition of man versus animals. Now a Messenger of Peace for the United Nations, Goodall does a great deal of philanthropic work focused on environmental conservationism and activism for animal welfare.

Stephen Hawking (1942–): a British theoretical physicist best known for his work regarding quantum gravity and black holes, as well his multiple contributions to popular science, including the record-breaking bestselling work *A Brief History of Time*. On August 12, 2009, Hawking—who is almost completely physically paralyzed by neuromuscular dystrophy—was granted the Presidential Medal of Freedom, the highest award the U.S. government can award to a civilian citizen.

THE Solar SYSTEM

THE SOLAR SYSTEM

The **sun** is so vital to us that it may be hard to believe that it is just an ordinary star, certainly on the big side, but still just one of more than 100 billion stars that make up our galaxy. A big sphere of ionized gas, mostly hydrogen and helium, the sun's diameter is 865,000 miles, and the temperature of its surface is approximately 10,000°F. At its core, the sun's temperature is thought to reach 27,000,000°F.

In our solar system, the sun is paramount. It is the closest star to the earth, and heat and light from the sun support every form of life on our planet. The sun's power, created by thermonuclear fusion, reaches to approximately 386 billion billion megawatts. The sun is much, much larger than any other object in our solar system, taking up 99.86 percent of the total mass.

The **moon**, the only natural satellite of the earth, orbits around our planet once a month and has an influence on us through its gravitational forces. The moon sets our timetables and affects many of the earth's cycles, in particular, the tides. In addition, the presence of the moon in our orbit helps to slow down the earth's rotation and stabilize its movement.

THE PLANETS

Our solar system is made up of eight planets, including Earth. Pluto was considered the ninth planet until August 2006, when the International Astronomical Union (IAU) officially changed the definition of a planet. Official planets now must do the following three things:

1. orbit around the sun
2. contain enough mass to allow it to achieve a round shape via gravity
3. clear "the neighborhood" around its orbit

Pluto does not clear other things out of its way, so along with Ceres and Eris, it has been named a *dwarf planet*. All three dwarf planets orbit the sun and are large enough for gravity to shape them into spheres, but none of them achieve the third criterion of clearing the neighborhood around their orbit.

VENUS

Venus
Venus is often called Earth's twin because the two of them are very similar in size. Venus is the planet that comes the closest to Earth, and when viewed from here, it is also the brightest—brighter than any other planet or star.

Diameter: 7,521 miles

Average distance from the sun: 67 million miles

Average surface temperature: 870°F

Number of moons: 0

Origin of name: the Roman goddess of love and beauty

Mercury
Mercury is the smallest, the densest, and the fastest planet and the closest planet to the sun. It has a very eccentric orbit and is the least explored of all the planets.

Diameter: 3,032 miles

Average distance from the sun: 36 million miles

Average surface temperature: 333°F

Number of moons: 0

Origin of name: the mythological Roman god of trade, travel, and thievery, famous for his speed

Earth

Earth
Although Earth is just one tiny planet in the vast universe, its precise distance from the sun—along with its abundance of water—enables it to also be home to all known life forms in the universe.

Diameter: 7,926 miles

Average distance from the sun: 93 million miles

Average surface temperature: 59°F

Number of moons: 1

Origin of name: a derivative of Old English *eorthe* and Germanic *erda* (Earth is the only planet whose English name does not come from Greek or Roman mythology.)

Mars
Mars is a red color, which inspired its nickname "the red planet," and an enduring favorite of science-fiction writers. Next to Earth, it has long been viewed as the most potentially inhabitable planet, but we have learned that its surface is far less welcoming than previously thought.

Diameter: 4,222 miles

Average distance from the sun: 142 million miles

Average surface temperature: −80°F

Number of moons: 2

Origin of name: the Roman god of war

When Were the Planets Discovered?

Mercury, Venus, Mars, Jupiter, and Saturn have been known about since ancient times—they can all be seen with the naked eye—and it is not known when exactly they were first discovered. Uranus was found to be a planet by William Herschel in 1781. Neptune was discovered in 1846 by Johann Galle and Heinrich Louis d'Arrest, although it is believed that Galileo located it long before, thinking it was a star in the field as he observed Jupiter. The distant Pluto was first discovered in 1930, but its status as one of the primary planets in the solar system only lasted until 2006.

NEPTUNE
URANUS
SATURN
JUPITER
MARS
THE SUN
EARTH
VENUS
MERCURY

Jupiter

Jupiter is by far the most massive planet in the solar system, being more than twice as large as all other planets combined. With its many satellites, several of them the size of planets themselves, Jupiter can appear to have its own miniature solar system.

Diameter: 88,846 miles

Average distance from the sun: 484 million miles

Average surface temperature: −230°F (at the top of Jupiter's clouds)

Number of moons: 63

Origin of name: king of the Roman gods

Saturn

Saturn, the second largest planet, is surrounded by seven flat rings. Jupiter, Neptune, and Uranus also have rings, but Saturn's are much brighter and more visible.

Diameter: 74,898 miles

Average distance from the sun: 886 million miles

Average surface temperature: −285°F (at the top of the clouds)

Number of satellites: 60

Origin of name: the Roman god of agriculture

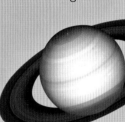

Uranus

Uranus was the first planet to be discovered in modern times (in 1781 by British astronomer William Herschel), with the help of a telescope. It had been located previously but thought to be a star.

Diameter: 31,763 miles

Average distance from the sun: 1.8 billion miles

Average surface temperature: −355°F (at the top of its atmosphere)

Number of satellites: 27

Origin of name: an ancient Greek deity of the heavens

Neptune

Neptune is a vivid blue color, due in part to methane in the atmosphere, although the reason the blue is so bright remains a mystery.

Diameter: 30,775 miles

Average distance from the sun: 2.8 billion miles

Average surface temperature: −370°F (at the top of its atmosphere)

Number of satellites: 13

Origin of name: the Roman god of the sea

SPACE

DWARF PLANETS

Pluto

Pluto used to be known as the smallest and coldest planet and the one farthest from the sun. It has not yet been visited by any spacecraft, but the plan is for the spacecraft *New Horizons* to reach it by 2015.

Diameter: 1,485 miles

Average distance from the sun: 3.6 billion miles

Average surface temperature: −380°F

Number of satellites: 3

Origin of name: the Roman god of the underworld

Ceres

Like Pluto, Ceres was also initially called a planet when it was first discovered in 1801. Later, it was considered the largest of all asteroids, before the three dwarf planets were decided upon in 2006. The name *Ceres* comes from the Roman goddess of the harvest and motherly love.

Eris

Eris is the largest of the dwarf planets and was discovered only in 2005 (from images shot in 2003). The discovery of Eris was the catalyst for the demotion of Pluto. As it is bigger than Pluto, either Eris was going to be named a new planet or Pluto had to be considered in a new light. Eris is the Greek and Roman goddess of strife and discord.

SPACE FIRSTS

First mission to space: the Russian *Sputnik 1* in 1957

First object to reach the surface of the moon: *Luna 2* in 1959

First man in space: Yuri Gagarin in 1961

First woman in space: Valentina Tereshkova in 1963

First animals in space: two fruit flies in 1946, then Laika the dog in 1951

First humans to walk on the moon: Neil Armstrong and Edwin "Buzz" Aldrin Jr. in 1969

HAVE YOU HEARD?

Astronauts can enjoy ketchup and mustard with their food in space, but any salt and pepper must be used in a liquid form only—in a zero-gravity situation, salt and pepper would float right into the air and could potentially get into an astronaut's eyes or nose, clog air vents, or contaminate equipment.

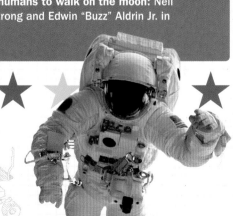

ROVER

GALILEO

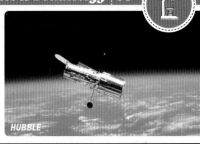
HUBBLE

NEIL ARMSTRONG (APOLLO 11)

KEY SPACECRAFTS

Sputnik: the first Soviet satellite sent into orbit around Earth in 1957

Explorer: the first U.S. satellite to orbit Earth in 1958

Pioneer: launched by the United States, the first space probes to travel through the asteroid belt and leave the solar system in 1972 and 1973 (*Pioneer 10* and *11*)

Mariner: NASA series of interplanetary probes sent to investigate Mars, Venus, and Mercury, and the first to take photos of and orbit another planet

Venera: Russian series of probes from 1961 to 1984 designed to study Venus

Apollo: NASA series of spacecrafts that accomplished the mission of putting a man on the moon

Skylab: U.S. first space station, in Earth's orbit from 1973 until 1979

Viking: NASA's two very successful space probes sent to Mars in 1975

Voyager: NASA's two space probes sent to study Jupiter and Saturn in 1977, which continued on into the outer solar system

Mir: record-holding Russian space station that was continuously inhabited by humans from 1986 until 2006

Phobos: Soviet series of probes sent to study Mars and its moons Phobos and Deimos

Magellan: space probe sent by NASA to Venus

Galileo: NASA spacecraft sent in 1989 to study Jupiter, where it landed six years later in 1995 and was the first spacecraft to orbit Jupiter and discover an asteroid's moon

Hubble: space telescope brought into orbit by the space shuttle in 1990 and the first to be serviced by astronauts in space

Space shuttle: NASA's Space Transportation System (STS) program of reusable spacecrafts for human missions into space, beginning with *Columbia,* which was completed in 1979

Mars Pathfinder: NASA program for planetary missions, launched in 1996 and landed on Mars in 1997

International Space Station: research facility currently under construction in orbit around Earth and the largest space station in history

HAVE YOU HEARD?

With the help of a robotic arm, a "porch" has been installed on the lab of the International Space Station so scientists can do outdoor experiments in the extreme environment of space.

THE AMAZING POWERS OF THE *HUBBLE SPACE TELESCOPE*

At 360 miles above our heads, working to repair the *Hubble Space Telescope*, NASA astronauts perform "brain surgery" in space, says astronaut John Grunsfeld, promising a brighter view of the cosmos for *Hubble* astronomers and fans alike.

These repairs improving the *Hubble* transform it "from a VW Super Beetle to a high-powered race car," says astronomer Julianne Dalcanton of the University of Washington in Seattle. *Hubble* will peer at stars and galaxies formed 500 million years after the Big Bang, armed with a new camera 30 times more sensitive to light and a chemical spectrometer 10 times more effective.

HUBBLE

A NEW ERA FOR STEM CELL RESEARCH

In 2009, President Obama ordered the National Institutes of Health (NIH) to issue guidelines removing the Bush administration's limits on human embryonic stem cell research funding.

Here are answers to common questions regarding the changes to come for stem cell research, based on interviews with researchers and policy experts.

Q: What are embryonic stem cells?
A: They are cells isolated from the early stages of embryo growth, which turn into almost all of the tissues of the body. At their early stage, however, they are unspecialized, with the potential to grow into any type of cell and to reproduce in large numbers.

Q: How are they collected?
A: Typically, couples donate excess embryos from fertility procedures to researchers. Researchers pull the 150 or so cells from inside one of these roughly six-day-old embryos, destroying it, and grow the cells in a lab.

Q: Why is this controversial?
A: Some religious groups, such as the U.S. Conference of Catholic Bishops, and political leaders, such as former president George W. Bush, have decried the death of the embryos.

Q: What dangers do opponents see in Obama's action?
A: The National Right to Life Committee says the order "opens door to human embryo farms," charging that researchers will start mass-harvesting embryos to create cell lines.

Q: What limits did Obama place, if any, on the stem cell lines that can now receive federal dollars for study?
A: Obama called for "appropriate safeguards," allowing research "only when it is both scientifically worthy and responsibly conducted. We will develop strict guidelines, which we will rigorously enforce, because we cannot ever tolerate misuse or abuse."

The NIH will take its cue from science organization guidelines that preclude cell lines gathered without informed consent or with inappropriate compensation of embryo donors.

Q: What benefits do researchers expect from studying more cell lines?
A: First, the opportunity to study disease-specific cell lines should give researchers insight into how these diseases originate in the body on a cellular level, shining light on the exact genetic defects behind diseases.

Second, cells can be cultured to screen for their response to drugs designed to address these defects, speeding pharmaceutical discoveries.

Third, an era of "regenerative medicine," in which patients get immune-system-friendly transplant organs might spring from stem cells. Geron Corporation in January received Food and Drug Administration clearance to begin testing of nerve stem cell injections of patients with spinal cord injuries.

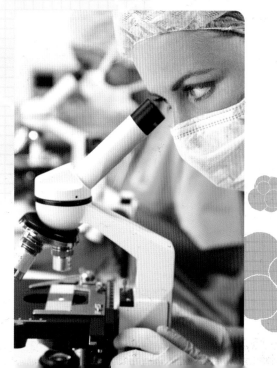

FLU PANDEMIC

FLU PANDEMIC

In June 2009, the World Health Organization (WHO) declared the first global influenza pandemic in 41 years as cases of H1N1 (known as *swine flu*) continued to mount in the United States, Europe, Latin America, and Australia. "The scientific criteria for a pandemic have been met," said Margaret Chan, director general of WHO. "The world is now at the start of the 2009 influenza pandemic."

WHO worked closely with vaccine makers, who geared up to produce the first doses of an H1N1 vaccine as soon as possible. Although Chan described the pandemic as "moderate in severity," she stressed that flu pandemics are unpredictable. "The virus writes the rules," she said. "This one, like all influenza viruses, can change the rules without rhyme or reason, at any time."

Centers for Disease Control and Prevention Director Thomas Frieden echoed Chan's assessment that the WHO announcement was more a reflection of the epidemic's geographic reach (affecting 74 countries and counting as of the announcement) than the virus's virulence. "This doesn't mean there's any difference in the level of severity of flu," he said. "This is not a flu that is anywhere near as severe as the 1918 flu, for example."

Frieden said federal, state, and local health officials have worked for years to prepare for a pandemic that many believed was inevitable. They have bought millions of doses of antiviral drugs for national stockpiles, prodded makers to vastly increase their capacity to produce flu vaccine, and staged desktop simulations to explore the best strategies for coping with an epidemic.

FLYING CAR TAKES OFF

In spring 2009, a flying car successfully zoomed above a small New York airport for 37 seconds, its creators said. The $194,000 carplane—aircar?—reached a height of 3,000 feet in the test flight, says Woburn, Massachusetts, parent company Terrafugia (terra-FOO-gee-ah).

The two-seat car is designed to take commuting to a whole new level. It can fly a distance of about 450 miles at speeds of 115 miles per hour, the company says. Converting to road use takes about 30 seconds.

More testing is required before these cars/planes go on sale, but CEO Carl Dietrich told the *Boston Globe* that he has already received $10,000 deposits from 40 potential buyers. They are expected to be ready for purchase in 2011.

USA TODAY Snapshots®

Youth movement on the Web

Percentage of people who keep a personal blog, display photos on the Web, or maintain their own Web site:

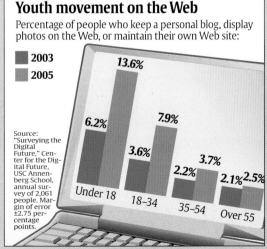

■ 2003
■ 2005

Under 18: 6.2%, 13.6%
18–34: 3.6%, 7.9%
35–54: 2.2%, 3.7%
Over 55: 2.1%, 2.5%

Source: "Surveying the Digital Future," Center for the Digital Future, USC Annenberg School, annual survey of 2,061 people. Margin of error ±2.75 percentage points.

By Cindy Clark and Marcy E. Mullins, USA TODAY

Steve Jobs: Widely viewed as the master marketer of his company, Apple, Steve Jobs is often given credit for developing the computer operating system that inspired Microsoft in its development and marketing of Windows. As cofounder of Apple, Jobs's credits include entertainment industry innovation through his part-ownership of the Pixar film studio, in which computer animation rivaled and, in many cases, exceeded older forms of the craft.

HAVE YOU HEARD? ★

THE INTERNET: THE MOST IMPORTANT POLITICAL TOOL

The campaign of President Barack Obama forever changed the landscape of politics. For the first time, a nominee harnessed the massive power of the Internet—from a top-notch social-networking site (myBarackObama.com) with more than 1.5 million accounts, to targeted e-mail initiatives, to strategic text messaging campaigns, to multiple Web pages and online action groups, to YouTube video messages, to iPhone and iPod touch applications, and beyond—to raise funds, organize supporters, and spread the candidate's message. The vision was powerful and hugely successful and will influence all significant political campaigns in the future.

Bill Gates: Bill Gates, one-half of the founding entrepreneurs of Microsoft, is one of the wealthiest men in the world. He is credited for the development, introduction, and mass acceptance of the Windows personal computing platform. In addition to creating the global health mega-charity The Bill & Melinda Gates Foundation, he has built a business empire that includes the Office suite of productivity products as well as Internet Explorer and the Xbox gaming systems.

COMPUTERS SURE HAVE CHANGED—HIGHLIGHTS THROUGHOUT HISTORY

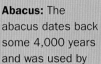
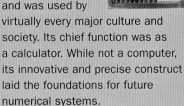

Generally speaking, a computer is something that remembers and conducts specific tasks without the need for human intervention. Though computers have played a role in the advancement of technology for the better part of the twentieth century, their history dates much further back. Here are some of those innovations and milestones in computing technology that have helped shape today's technological landscape.

Abacus: The abacus dates back some 4,000 years and was used by virtually every major culture and society. Its chief function was as a calculator. While not a computer, its innovative and precise construct laid the foundations for future numerical systems.

Vacuum tube: The vacuum tube is an electronic component developed in the late 1800s. It was constructed so that the vacuum would allow for the unobstructed flow of electrons between two points. It was most famously seen in the form of early light bulbs and helped usher in the electrical revolution in the world's major cities. It is the foundation for today's solid-state switches and circuitry.

Transistor: The transistor is an electronic device first developed in the 1920s and still in use today. It replaced the vacuum tube as the primary means of opening and closing switches and, interestingly, its size allows for millions of transistors to be on one microprocessor alone.

Konrad Zuse's Z1: The first of the real computers, developed in 1938, this is often grouped with the Atanosoff-Berry Computer and ENIAC (Electronic Numerical Integrator and Computer) in discussions of the world's first computers. While it lacked the impressive capabilities of ENIAC, it, nonetheless, offered formidable computing power. However, electronic computers would soon come to dominate the technology landscape.

ENIAC: The Electronic Numerical Integrator and Computer, or ENIAC, was the world's first and fastest electronic computer, was developed by the United States in 1946. It could compute 5,000 computations in one second, unheard of at the time. Its primary use, which was for the military, was to aid in the calculation of tables for artillery shelling trajectories as well as to solve mathematical problems related to the development of nuclear weaponry.

Atanosoff-Berry Computer: The Atanosoff-Berry Computer (ABC) was developed in the 1940s in the United States and while an achievement, it was quickly surpassed by faster, more powerful computers. Its reliance on linear computations led to its retirement, though its ability to perform multiple computations was heralded at the time.

Integrated circuit (the "chip"): Integrated circuits, or ICs, are complex electronic devices that perform multiple tasks or calculations in far less than one second. Today's ICs are so small yet perform millions of tasks daily. Though most people would know an IC as a microprocessor used in today's computers, ICs can also be found in appliances and automobiles.

Microprocessor: Since their mass introduction in the 1970s, the microprocessor has been used in a number of products, most notably in today's complex central processing units (CPUs) used to drive the operations of personal computers.

Floppy disk: The floppy disk was given its name because of the magnetic film used in its construction, which was extremely flexible yet delicate. To the eye, it looked less like a round disk but more like a square, which was the shape of its case to protect it from damage. I became widesprea in the 1980s and was used as a data storage medium for early personal computers. It has since been replaced by flash drives, which are more durable and hold more memory.

IBM personal computer: The introduction of the IBM PC in 1981 ushered in the personal computer age for consumers and was the beginning of an industry that continues to innovate and evolve. Constructed of Intel CPUs and run by MS-DOS, the IBM PC predates the Apple Macintosh, released in 1984. Interestingly, IBM left the PC business and, with some irony, licensed its software from Bill Gates and Microsoft, which led to its demise as a PC software innovator and allowed Windows to be the global market leader in desktop software.

Laptop computer:
Current laptop computers reflect continued innovation, through size and portability, in the personal computing industry. Laptops are in use by most households, given their convenience and near-desktop-computing capacity. Sized to fold like a textbook, they usually have two sides, one with a screen and the other with a full keyboard.

Apple Macintosh: The first commercially successful computer sold by Apple, in 1984, the Macintosh added innovations in use today, like the mouse and an easy-to-use graphical user interface (GUI). It was the first computer marketed with a cutting-edge television commercial, using George Orwell's *1984* as a backdrop for the ad. It was also unique in that it was simply called Macintosh, in homage to the company's corporate name of Apple.

Handheld PDA: The PDA, or personal digital assistant, is viewed as the basis for today's iPhone and owes its heritage to the Palm Pilot, which revolutionized the use of handheld, albeit limited, computing devices.

iPod: Innovated and marketed by Apple, the iPod—in a derivative of mp3 players—revolutionized the portable music player. Since its introduction in 2001, millions have sold world-wide, and both its size and capabilities have evolved beyond that of a music player to include multimedia and more advanced computing applications.

iPhone: The iPhone is the modern culmination of handheld computer, entertainment center, and fashion statement. At its core, it owes its lineage to the iPod but more appropriately resembles a multifunction lifestyle device. In partnership with AT&T, with whom the product was introduced, the iPhone made the selection of a mobile phone more personal-statement driven, with tens of thousands of applications available for download from Apple.

E-reader: A tablet-like reading device, today's e-book readers are the beginning of the publishing industry's move into the digital age. Its ease of use, coupled with enough memory to hold multiple books and wireless capabilities—allowing users to access online books for quick download and with significant savings over printed versions—make it increasingly popular with readers.

IPHONE

NOOK

Sports

THE MAJOR LEAGUES

MLB

Major League Baseball

Major League Baseball is made of two leagues: the National League (founded in 1876) and the American League (founded in 1901). In 1903, the two leagues began working together, and in 1920, they combined their administrative structures, working from then on under one commissioner. The leagues include 29 teams in the United States and 1 in Canada.

LeBRON JAMES

National Football League

The National Football League was founded in 1920 and merged with the American Football League in 1970. It includes 32 teams in the United States. Canada has its own football league with different rules.

National Basketball Association

The National Basketball Association was founded as the Basketball Association of America in 1946 and then changed its name in 1949 when it took over the National Basketball League. The NBA includes 29 teams in the United States and 1 in Canada.

DAVID BECKHAM

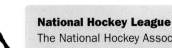

National Hockey League

The National Hockey Association was founded in 1909 and then changed into the National Hockey League in 1917. It includes 30 teams from the United States and Canada.

TEEN CHOICE AWARDS— SPORTS FAVORITES (2009)

Action Sports Athletes,
Female: Stephanie Gilmore, surfer
Shawn Johnson, gymnast

Male: Ryan Sheckler, skateboarder
David Beckham, soccer player

HAVE YOU HEARD? ★

Based on attendance per game, The National Football League is the most popular professional sports league in the world. The Super Bowl is the most watched annual event on U.S. television.

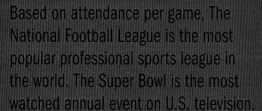

QUITE A TRIP!

QUITE A TRIP!

A 17-year-old Los Angeles–area teen was hailed as the youngest person to sail around the world alone.

Zac Sunderland docked at Marina del Rey 13 months after setting off in his 36-foot sailboat, *Intrepid*. He was 16 when he began the 28,000-mile journey on June 14, 2008, and the first person to complete it before turning 18.

The previous record holder was Australian Jesse Martin, who was 18 when he finished his voyage in 1999.

NFL

THE BIGGEST OF THE MAJOR LEAGUES

Who are some of the most dominant major league franchises of all time?

Los Angeles Lakers: They have won 15 NBA championships in their 61 seasons (24.6%) in Los Angeles and Minneapolis.

New York Yankees: They have won 26 of 104 (25 %) World Series, including four titles in five years from 1996 to 2000.

Montreal Canadiens: They have won 23 of 91 (25.3 %) Stanley Cups in NHL history. However, they haven't won since 1993, the longest drought in franchise history.

Boston Celtics: They have won 17 of 63 (27%) NBA championships and beat the Lakers in last year's NBA Finals, ending a 21-season title drought, longest in franchise history.

Green Bay Packers: They won 8 of 37 (21.6%) NFL championships from 1933 to 1969, before the 1970 AFL-NFL merger. They were so dominant in the 1960s that the Super Bowl prize is named the Vince Lombardi Trophy, after their coach.

Pittsburgh Steelers: They beat the Arizona Cardinals in Super Bowl XLIII, in 2009, their sixth Super Bowl in 39 seasons (15.4%) since the 1970 AFL-NFL merger. They've also had only three coaches since 1969, and all three won titles: Chuck Noll, Bill Cowher, and Mike Tomlin.

STEELERS

HAVE YOU HEARD of THESE WILD SPORTS?

Wife carrying started in Finland and is an actual race in which a male carries his female teammate through an obstacle course to the finish line. Major competitions can be found in Finland, Wisconsin, and Michigan, among other spots.

Zorb ball, or globe-riding, created in New Zealand, is the wild activity of bumping and rolling down a hill inside a huge transparent inflatable ball.

Bog snorkeling is an event in which competitors suit up in snorkels and flippers and swim along murky trenches cut into peat bogs. Every August in Wales, you can attend the World Bog Snorkeling Championships.

UNDERWATER HOCKEY

Underwater hockey (also known as octopush) involves two teams working to send a hockey puck across the bottom of a swimming pool and into the right goal, and has been embraced by countries such as Canada, the United Kingdom, Australia, New Zealand, and South Africa.

Shin kicking, created centuries ago in England and still played to this day, is exactly what it sounds like: two people kick each other in the shins until the pain brings one of them to the ground, causing the opponent to win that round.

Chess boxing is a sport with a rare level of communion between physical and intellectual strength. Competitors go through alternating, carefully timed rounds of both chess and boxing. There is an actual World Chess Boxing Organization, whose motto is "Fighting is done in the ring and wars are waged on the board."

Cheese rolling is a sport in which a large round of Double Gloucester cheese is rolled down a hill and chased by a number of competitors. The ultimate goal is to catch the cheese, but this is rarely possible—the cheese is given a one-second head start and rolls surprisingly quickly. So, the first one across the finish line wins the prize: the cheese that has beaten them all to the bottom.

Extreme ironing was started in the United Kingdom in 1997, and is now played all over the world, from Taiwan to Canada to Madagascar. It involves taking an iron and ironing board (if you can) and ironing some laundry in an extreme location, like while climbing a mountain or doing an underwater dive. ExtremeIroning.com describes it as "an outdoor activity that combines the danger and excitement of an extreme sport with the satisfaction of a well-pressed shirt."

VANCOUVER

OLYMPIC SUMMER GAMES

Athens	1896
Paris	1900
St. Louis	1904
London	1908
Stockholm	1912
Antwerp	1920
Paris	1924
Amsterdam	1928
Los Angeles	1932
Berlin	1936
London	1948
Helsinki	1952
Melbourne/Stockholm	1956
Rome	1960
Tokyo	1964
Mexico	1968
Munich	1972
Montreal	1976
Moscow	1980
Los Angeles	1984
Seoul	1988
Barcelona	1992
Atlanta	1996
Sydney	2000
Athens	2004
Beijing	2008
upcoming: London	2012

SHAUN WHITE

OLYMPIC WINTER GAMES

THE OLYMPICS

The modern **Olympic Games**, established in 1896, were inspired by the **ancient Olympic Games** in Olympia, Greece, that first took place in 776 BC. The modern games are the world's largest and most popular international sports events. They take place every two years, alternating between the **Summer and Winter Olympic Games** and featuring many thousands of athletes at the top of their game from almost every nation in the world. The spirit of the Olympics is one of universality and peaceful competition among nations, a concept that also originated with the Games in ancient Greece, when warring Greek cities came together in peace for the Games. The International Olympic Committee (IOC), founded in 1894, created the **Olympic Truce** to revive and carry on this tradition.

The Games have evolved and changed quite a bit over time. With an event this global and monumental, corporate sponsorship and the media have come to play a significant role in the production. The **host city**, chosen for each game by the IOC, is responsible for creating and financing an elaborate celebration worthy of the momentous occasion. Cities across the world compete fiercely for the opportunity to host the Olympics, and the massive international exposure and promotion that come along with it.

Chamonix	1924
St. Moritz	1928
Lake Placid	1932
Garmisch-Partenkirchen	1936
St. Moritz	1948
Oslo	1952
Cortina d'Ampezzo	1956
Squaw Valley	1960
Innsbruck	1964
Grenoble	1968
Sapporo	1972
Innsbruck	1976
Lake Placid	1980
Sarajevo	1984
Calgary	1988
Albertville	1992
Lillehammer	1994
Nagano	1998
Salt Lake City	2002
Turin	2006
Vancouver	2010
upcoming: Sochi	2014

PARALYMPICS

PARALYMPICS

The **Paralympic Games** are elite, international sporting events for athletes with a variety of disabilities. Created in 1960, the Paralympic Games have grown from 400 athletes in Rome that first year to more than 4,000 athletes today. Like the Olympics, they happen ever two years and are divided into alternating summer and winter competitions. The focus of these games has always been on the top-level athletic achievement of the participants, not on their disabilities.

SPECIAL OLYMPICS

The **Special Olympics World Games**, also held every two years with alternating summer and winter competitions, are international sporting events for athletes with intellectual disabilities. The first Special Olympics Games took place in 1968, inspired and popularized by the passionate work of the late Eunice Kennedy Shriver.

YOUTH OLYMPIC GAMES

The Youth Olympic Games are international sporting events designed to feature top-level athletes from ages 14 to 18. They will take place every two years, alternating between summer and winter competitions, with a strong focus on education and culture among all participants.

Special Olympics

AUTO RACING

NASCAR

With stock-car racing becoming more and more popular following the second World War, Bill France Sr. of Daytona Beach, Florida, decided that the sport needed more organization and called a meeting in 1947. In that meeting, NASCAR (the National Association for Stock Car Auto Racing) was formed.

The first NASCAR-sanctioned race was held in 1948, with the Cup series (now the Sprint Cup) beginning in 1949.

NASCAR states that its constants have been, and always will be: "Close, safe competition, fair stewardship and drivers who are genuine American heroes."

INDIANAPOLIS 500

Founded in 1911, the Indy 500 happens every Memorial Day weekend at the Indianapolis Motor Speedway in Speedway, Indiana. One of the ultimate auto racing events in the world, it features open-wheel race cars instead of stock cars and many unique traditions all its own. For example: the final few weeks of practice leading up to the race are always referred to as "the month of May"; peanuts in the concession stands are considered bad luck; and the winner drinks milk right after the race as a part of the victory celebration. In 2009, Brazilian racer Helio Castroneves won for the third year in a row.

JIMMIE JOHNSON MAKES NASCAR HISTORY

As he made Sprint Cup history November 22, 2009, at Homestead-Miami Speedway, Jimmie Johnson (FSY) had a clear view of those poised to keep him out of the record books in the future.

With a fifth-place finish in the Ford 400, the Hendrick Motorsports star became the first to win four consecutive titles in NASCAR's premier series and joined Dale Earnhardt, Richard Petty and Jeff Gordon (FSY) as the only drivers with more than three championships.

"To think about the greats before me and this is something none of them have done, it's unbelievable," said Johnson, whose No. 48 Chevrolet finished behind the cars of Denny Hamlin, Jeff Burton, Kevin Harvick, and Kurt Busch.

All have flashed plenty of late-season momentum, but Hamlin was the first to throw down the gauntlet after his fourth victory of 2009 — doubling his previous single-season best.

"I promise the next couple of years we're going to win the championship," the Joe Gibbs Racing driver said after climbing from his No. 11 Toyota. "(Johnson has) been the standard, and that's who we want to beat."

Johnson, who finished 141 points ahead of teammate Mark Martin (FSY) (now a five-time title runner-up), vowed the same.

Major League Baseball

BASEBALL

YANKEES WIN THEIR 27TH TITLE

The Yankees won their 27th World Series title in November, 2009, dethroning the Philadelphia Phillies 7-3, bringing their tradition across the street to new Yankee Stadium and adding a seventh crown for ailing 79-year-old owner George Steinbrenner.

A NEW BASEBALL CLASSIC

There's one very basic description for the new $1.5 billion Yankee Stadium, an element that wasn't in the architectural drawings per se but was clearly integral to the plan.

"We wanted . . . to create a stadium that, when you go in, there's a "wow" factor to it," Yankees President Randy Levine says. "It's going to be nothing like anything in baseball and nothing like anything in sports," says first baseman Mark Teixeira.

The Yankees' new home is grand in scale, with about 60 percent more square footage than in the previous stadium. The added space includes 4 merchandise stores, 56 private luxury suites, and 13 restaurants-lounges-food courts.

The playing surface? The field dimensions are identical to the renovated Yankee Stadium that opened in 1976, but home plate is 20 feet closer to the backstop to put fans closer to the action.

The players clubhouse? About 30,000 square feet of amenities, from a computer at each locker to televisions . . . in the washrooms.

The fans don't feel cheated: About 1,400 TV monitors are in the building. Among them are monitors positioned near every seat that doesn't have a full view of the center-field video scoreboard.

Nostalgic touches all around

In one respect, the new Yankee Stadium was 86 years in the making. The exterior is patterned after the original stadium that opened in 1923, and the interior includes several touches designed to reflect the charm of the "House That Ruth Built."

"We wanted, in effect, to return to our history," Levine says.

The iconic frieze (commonly called the facade by fans) again rings the grandstand.

The numbering of the sections is the same as in the original park, and the monuments are back in center field (though not in the field of play).

Field-level auxiliary scoreboards, like the originals recognizable to generations from the historic photo from Don Larsen's perfect game in the 1956 World Series, are placed in left-center and right-center.

Photo displays abound throughout the stadium, connecting fans to the Yankees' rich history.

Large images of the championship teams are hung above the concession stands on the main level; a display board by the bleacher's gate features a tribute to catcher Yogi Berra and his "Yogi-isms"; and special photos of Yankees MVPs move from silhouette to full image near the press box.

"We consider this whole building to be a museum," Lonn Trost, the Yankees' chief operating officer, says, "a living museum not just to the Yankees but baseball in general."

SOCCER

2009 FIFA WORLD CUP (FÉDÉRATION INTERNATIONALE DE FOOTBALL ASSOCIATION)
Founded: 1930

2009 Champions: Italy (fourth title)

2009 FIFA WOMEN'S WORLD CUP
Founded: 1991

2009 Champions: Germany

→ THE MLS CUP

Major League Soccer has its most improbable champion in its fourteen-year history.

Real Salt Lake, a small-market expansion team that dealt with a harsh political landscape to survive in Utah and scraped into the MLS playoffs, won the league championship on penalty kicks after a 1-1 draw in 2009 with the Los Angeles Galaxy before a festive crowd of 46,011 fans.

Robbie Russell, a part-time starting defender for Real, hit the winning penalty kick. Nick Rimando, who stopped three penalty kicks in the semifinal win against the Chicago Fire, turned away two more Sunday and was named the game's most outstanding player.

Though its regular-season record (11-12-7) was barely enough to clinch the final berth in the playoffs, Real Salt Lake outplayed the Galaxy through most of the final, dominating play in the second half and extra time.

It was the second MLS Cup final decided by penalty kicks. The first was in 2006, when the Houston Dynamo beat the New England Revolution.

BASKETBALL
PRO

2009 NBA CHAMPIONSHIP SERIES

In the NBA Championship series of the 2008–09 NBA season, the Los Angeles Lakers beat the Orlando Magic four games to one. The Lakers' coach was Phil Jackson and team captain was Kobe Bryant. The Magic's coach was Stan Van Gundy and team captain was Dwight Howard. Kobe Bryant was named the series MVP.

HAVE YOU HEARD?

Popular basketball superstar LeBron James, who has broken many records and plays for the Cleveland Cavaliers, excels at something else in addition to basketball: working to have a positive impact on the lives of young kids. A dad of two young sons himself, James works with Nickelodeon and its Big Green Help campaign to raise awareness about both the environment and the importance of exercise. James, who sees himself as still very much a kid at heart, is using his influence as an All-Star sports hero to encourage kids to get outside, ride bikes, play sports, be healthy, and engage themselves in what's going on in the world.

KOBE

KOBE BRYANT

THE KING

LeBRON JAMES

COLLEGE

2009 NCAA MEN'S DIVISION 1 BASKETBALL TOURNAMENT

Finals site: Ford Field, Detroit, Michigan

Champions: North Carolina (89-72)

Runners-up: Michigan State

MOP: Wayne Ellington, North Carolina

QUITE A GAME!

From the start of the game against Michigan State, it was clear North Carolina (34-4) was in a league of its own.

The Tar Heels set an NCAA title-game record with a 21-point halftime lead, eclipsing the previous halftime record lead of 18 set by champion Ohio State against California in 1960 and matched seven years later by UCLA against Dayton.

In staking a 55-34 lead at intermission, UNC set a first-half title game record for points, breaking the 2003 mark of 53 Syracuse set in beating Kansas.

For good measure, star point guard Ty Lawson tied an NCAA championship game record with seven steals—by halftime. He finished with eight steals to go with his game-high 21 points.

This is UNC's fifth national title, tying Indiana for third all time behind UCLA's eleven titles and Kentucky's seven. It is the second championship for coach Roy Williams, who won his first four years ago.

The victory gave four-time All-American forward Tyler Hansbrough a storybook finish, capping one of the most illustrious careers for a four-year college player.

"All year long, everyone anointed this team," Williams said during the trophy presentation. "They handled injuries and they handled losses . . . I'm the luckiest coach in America."

Hansbrough, who scored 18, departs as the Atlantic Coast Conference (ACC) all-time leading scorer with 2,872 points. He is the school's leading rebounder with 1,219. UNC will retire his jersey alongside those of former stars such as Michael Jordan, James Worthy, and Phil Ford.

Jordan was in Detroit for this show, along with Michigan State alumnus Earvin "Magic" Johnson, who led MSU to its first national title in 1979. Jordan, the headliner of a five-member Naismith Hall of Fame class, led UNC to the 1982 title under coach Dean Smith.

Johnson and Larry Bird of one-hit wonder Indiana State met in the '79 title game and ceremoniously presented the game ball Monday in honor of the thirtieth anniversary of their meeting.

On a night when some of the game's greats were in the house, UNC gave a five-star performance.

TYLER HANSBROUGH

FOOTBALL

PRO

NFL 2009 REGULAR SEASON LEAGUE LEADERS

	NAME	TEAM	YARDS
PASSING	1. Matt Schaub	Houston Texans	4,770
	2. Peyton Manning	Indianapolis Colts	4,500
	3. Tony Romo	Dallas Cowboys	4,483
RUSHING	1. Chris Johnson	Tennessee Titans	2,006
	2. Steven Jackson	St. Louis Rams	1,416
	3. Thomas Jones	New York Jets	1,402
RECEIVING	1. Andre Johnson	Houston Texans	1,569
	2. Wes Welker	New England Patriots	1,348
	3. Miles Austin	Dallas Cowboys	1,320

2009 SUPER BOWL XLIII

Stadium: Raymond James Stadium, Tampa, Florida

Winners: Pittsburgh Steelers, 27 points

Opponents: Arizona Cardinals, 23 points

MVP: Santonio Holmes, Pittsburgh Steelers, wide receiver

COLLEGE

USA TODAY COACHES' POLL PICKS FOR TOP COLLEGE FOOTBALL TEAM (LAST 10 YEARS)

SEASON	SCHOOL	HEAD COACH
2000	Oklahoma	Bob Stoops
2001	Miami	Larry Coker
2002	Ohio State	Jim Tressel
2003	LSU	Nick Saban
2004	USC	Pete Carroll
2005	Texas	Mack Brown
2006	Florida	Urban Meyer
2007	LSU	Les Miles
2008	Florida	Urban Meyer
2009	Alabama	Nick Saban

X-GAMES GO GREEN

X Games Environmentality (XGE) is a program that puts environmental initiatives at the forefront of all planning for the X Games, making them a true leader in hosting environmentally responsible sporting events. As described on their Web site (XGamesEnvironmentality.com), they minimize the impact of each event through

- waste minimization
- use of renewable resources
- purchase of environmentally conscious products, and
- pollution prevention.

They have an extensive recycling and composting program, create incentives for fans who rideshare to events, and after X Games 13 (the world's greenest action-sports event ever), they even planted 2,000 trees in Colorado's Pike–San Isabel National Forest on behalf of each athlete, staff, and media member who participated in the event.

HOCKEY

2009 STANLEY CUP

Winners: Pittsburgh Penguins
(Eastern Conference champions)

Opponents: Detroit Red Wings
(Western Conference champions)

MVP: Evgeni Malkin

GOLF

MEN

MASTERS

Established: 1934

Course: Augusta National Golf Club,
Augusta, Georgia

2009 Champion: Angel Cabrera

PHIL MICKELSON

U.S. OPEN

Established: 1895

2009 Champion: Lucas Glover

PGA CHAMPIONSHIP DUEL

CBS touted the 2009 PGA Championship as "Glory's Last Shot."

Who knew it would be underdog Y. E. Yang who'd emerge with the laurels as he beat world No. 1 golfer Tiger Woods and became the first Asian player to win one of golf's four major championships?

Woods lost for the first time in a major when he entered the final round with the lead.

WOMEN

U.S. WOMEN'S OPEN

Established: 1946

2009 Champion: Eun-Hee Ji

LPGA CHAMPIONSHIP

Established: 1955

2009 Champion: Anna Nordqvist

MICHELLE WIE

TENNIS

AUSTRALIAN OPEN 2009

Men's Singles: Rafael Nadal

Women's Singles: Serena Williams

2009 FRENCH OPEN

Men's Singles: Roger Federer

Women's Singles: Svetlana Kuznetsova

WIMBLEDON 2009

Men's Singles: Roger Federer

Women's Singles: Serena Williams

RAFEAL NADAL

U.S. OPEN 2009

Men's Singles: Juan Martin del Potro

Women's Singles: Kim Clijsters

ROGER FEDERER

TENNIS STAR MISSES A FEW

Swiss tennis sensation **Roger Federer** continues to dominate the professional tennis scene, and holds the impressive record for more Grand Slam singles titles than any other male player (15 titles by September 2009). But he is no longer completely unbeatable: Spanish tennis star **Rafael Nadal** can hold his own against Federer like no other player, and dethroned the five-time Wimbledon champion in 2008. And Chilean **Juan Martín del Potro** defeated Federer in the 2009 U.S. Open, after Federer had reigned as champion of that tournament as well for the previous five years.

★ HAVE YOU HEARD?

Andy Roddick is known for his big serve, and he has the record for fastest serve (155 mph).

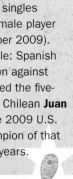

United States

THE FLAG

WHO MAKES UP THE POPULATION?

According to the U.S. Census Bureau, there are 304,059,724 people living in the United States (and that number is growing over time)!

Religious affiliations: The primary religion in the United States is Christianity, with 75 percent of the population identifying themselves as Christian. Approximately 4 percent of Americans practice non-Christian religions, including Judaism, Buddhism, Mormonism, Islam, and others, while at least 15 percent see themselves as having no particular religious identity.

Language: The United States does not actually have an official national language, but the majority of Americans—about 82 percent—speak American English as their first language. The second most spoken language in the United States is Spanish—more than 12 percent of Americans speak it as their native language. Other popular languages spoken and used (mostly by immigrant populations) in the United States include Chinese, French, German, Tagalog (a Philippine language), Vietnamese, Italian, Korean, Arabic, Japanese, Polish, Greek, Russian, French Creole, Native American dialects, and many others.

Chicago

FAST FACTS

Biggest state: Alaska

Smallest state: Rhode Island

Highest mountain: Mount McKinley, Alaska

Lowest point: Death Valley, California

Deepest lake: Crater Lake, Oregon

Tallest building: Willis Tower (formerly named Sears Tower), Chicago, Illinois

United States

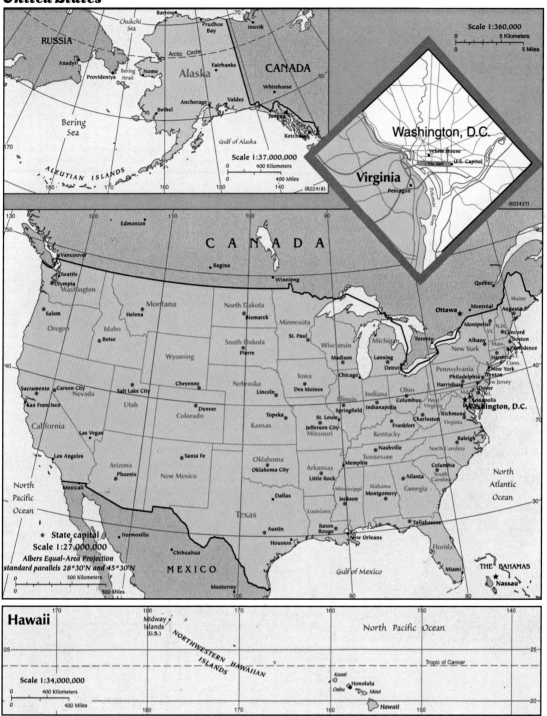

Barrow
Chukchi Sea
Prudhoe Bay
Inuvik
RUSSIA
Arctic Circle
Anadyr
Providenlya
Bering Strait
Nome
Alaska
Fairbanks
CANADA
Whitehorse
Bethel
Anchorage
Valdez
Juneau
Bering Sea
Gulf of Alaska
Ketchikan
ALEUTIAN ISLANDS

Scale 1:37,000,000
0 400 Kilometers
0 400 Miles
(R02418)

Scale 1:360,000
0 5 Kilometers
0 5 Miles

Washington, D.C.
White House
The Mall
U.S. Capitol
Virginia
Pentagon
Potomac River
(R02437)

Edmonton
CANADA
Vancouver
Regina
Seattle
Winnipeg
Olympia
Washington
Québec
Montana
North Dakota
Minnesota
Maine
Salem
Helena
Bismarck
Ottawa
Montréal
Augusta
Oregon
Idaho
South Dakota
St. Paul
Wisconsin
Michigan
Toronto
Montpelier
N.H.
Concord
Boston
Boise
Pierre
Madison
Lansing
Albany
Mass.
Providence
R.I.
Wyoming
Iowa
Chicago
Detroit
New York
Hartford
Conn.
Sacramento
Carson City
Salt Lake City
Cheyenne
Nebraska
Des Moines
Pennsylvania
New York
Trenton
Nevada
Lincoln
Illinois
Indiana
Ohio
Philadelphia
N.J.
San Francisco
Utah
Denver
Harrisburg
Dover
Del.
California
Colorado
Topeka
St. Louis
Springfield
Indianapolis
Columbus
West Virginia
Richmond
Annapolis
Md.
Washington, D.C.
Las Vegas
Kansas
Jefferson City
Missouri
Frankfort
Virginia
Los Angeles
Santa Fe
Kentucky
Raleigh
Arizona
Oklahoma
Nashville
North Carolina
Phoenix
New Mexico
Oklahoma City
Arkansas
Tennessee
Columbia
North Atlantic Ocean
Mexicali
Little Rock
Memphis
South Carolina
North Pacific Ocean
Dallas
Mississippi
Alabama
Georgia
Atlanta
Jackson
Montgomery
State capital
Scale 1:27,000,000
Albers Equal-Area Projection
standard parallels 28°30'N and 45°30'N
0 500 Kilometers
0 500 Miles
Hermosillo
Texas
Austin
Louisiana
Baton Rouge
New Orleans
Tallahassee
Florida
Houston
Chihuahua
MEXICO
Monterrey
Gulf of Mexico
Miami
THE BAHAMAS
Nassau

Hawaii
Midway Islands (U.S.)
NORTHWESTERN HAWAIIAN ISLANDS
North Pacific Ocean
Tropic of Cancer
Scale 1:34,000,000
0 400 Kilometers
0 400 Miles
Kauai
Oahu
Honolulu
Maui
Hawaii

U.S.

THE ARMED FORCES

The U.S. armed forces were originally created in 1775 to defend the burgeoning nation in the Revolutionary War against the British Empire. The forces went through various stages of upheaval until 1787, when the Constitution gave Congress and the president the power to organize, support, and govern over the military. Today, the United States maintains its long history of a military under primarily civilian control and powered almost entirely (and exclusively since 1972) by volunteers.

The U.S. armed forces, among the largest in the world, are strong, well-trained, and equipped with the most advanced and powerful tools available. On the official U.S. government Web site, whitehouse.gov, the list of primary areas of focus for the U.S. military includes the following:

- **Irregular warfare capabilities:** to increase intelligence, surveillance, and reconnaissance (ISR) support and expand special operations capabilities

- **Air supremacy:** to preserve and improve upon the U.S. unparalleled airpower capabilities

- **Dominance at sea:** to support our naval forces, replace older ships, modernize naval capabilities, and give more support to coastal regions

- **Missile defense:** to increase our missile defense capabilities to better protect U.S. forces and those of its allies

- **Space:** to work with allies to continue technological advancements and allied space capabilities

- **Cyberspace:** to work on both the domestic and international fronts to ensure the security of global information within a functioning and protected cyber domain

The United States is also increasingly invested in supporting not only the troops but also the military families and veterans who make up a vital but sometimes neglected piece of the military picture.

ARMED FORCES

"THIS IS YOUR VICTORY"

In November 2008, Barack Obama, who introduced himself to the nation four years prior as "a skinny kid with a funny name," celebrated his election as the first African American president of the United States. On the shore of Lake Michigan in Chicago, before a multiracial crowd of 125,000, Obama told his supporters: "It belongs to you. This is your victory."

For Obama, a first-term senator with family connections that span the globe from Kenya to Kansas, it was the dizzying conclusion to an unlikely odyssey that began in the snow of February 2007, when he announced his candidacy near the Illinois statehouse where Abraham Lincoln, the nation's sixteenth president, served as a legislator.

A virtually unknown state legislator when he spoke to the Democratic National Convention in 2004, Obama galvanized viewers by turning his own struggle to come to grips with his biracial identity into a metaphor for the nation's need to rise above its divisions.

He echoed that theme again in his election night speech, calling on Americans to rise above "the partisan pettiness and immaturity that has poisoned our politics."

"In this country, we rise or fall as one nation," Obama said.

MAJOR U.S. RESOURCES

The United States is the world's top producer of electrical and nuclear energy, liquid natural gas, sulfur, phosphates, and salt. We are also the number one producer of corn and soy beans and home to the two most well-known brands in the world: Coca-Cola and McDonald's. The United States is also the third biggest producer of oil in the world, in addition to being its largest importer.

MAJOR U.S. INDUSTRIES

The top export commodity of the United States is electrical machinery, and the top import is motor vehicles. The leading business fields are wholesale and retail trade, finance, and insurance, and the top manufacturing area is chemical products.

HAVE YOU HEARD?

One out of every fifty American children experiences homelessness at some point, and far too few state homeless shelters cater to families with children. A 2009 report released by the National Center on Family Homelessness emphasizes the long-term damage a period of homelessness can create for a child but focuses on action plans designed in the hope to end homelessness for all U.S. children within the next ten years.

"In this country, we rise or fall as one nation."

WELL-KNOWN U.S. ACTIVISTS

Clara Barton: Clara (Clarissa) Barton lived from 1821 (she was born on Christmas day) to 1912. She was a nurse and established the American Red Cross, which began as an agency to get supplies to wounded soldiers and became, under her leadership, an international relief organization for worldwide disasters. She also worked with Susan B. Anthony on the suffrage movement, as well as with Frederick Douglass to end slavery.

REEVE

Christopher Reeve: Christopher Reeve lived from 1952 to 2004. He was an American actor, film director, director, producer, and screenwriter. He is most remembered for his role as Superman. In 1995 he was thrown from the horse he was riding in a competition and left a quadriplegic. Reeve spent the rest of his life advocating for stem cell research to help others with spinal cord injuries.

Harriet Tubman: Harriet Tubman lived from 1822 to 1913. She was born into slavery and escaped. She then made thirteen rescue missions to help more than 70 other slaves escape through a network of antislavery activists known as the Underground Railroad. After the American Civil War, she fought the right for women to vote (suffrage).

Martin Luther King Jr.: Rev. Dr. Martin Luther King Jr. was born in 1929 on January 15, a day now known as Martin Luther King Day, and was killed in 1968. He was a Baptist minister and leader in the civil rights movement. He is famous for his "I Have a Dream" speech, which he gave at the March on Washington (in which the theme was jobs and freedom for African Americans) in 1963. In 1964, he received the Nobel Peace Prize, the youngest person ever to do so.

"I HAVE A DREAM"

RED CROSS

Al Gore: Albert Arnold "Al" Gore Jr. was born in 1948. He was the forty-fifth vice president of the United States from 1993 to 2001 under Bill Clinton. Gore is an environmental activist, raising awareness of global warming. He ran for president in 2000 against George W. Bush, winning the popular vote but not the electoral college, in a decision that was ultimately decided by the Supreme Court.

Michael J. Fox: Michael J. Fox was born in Canada in 1961 and became an American actor best known for his roles in the *Back to the Future* trilogy and his TV role on *Family Ties*. In 1991, he was diagnosed with Parkinson's disease and went public with that fact in 1998. Since that time he has been a passionate advocate for finding a cure.

KIDS MAKING A DIFFERENCE

KIDS MAKING A DIFFERENCE

Zach Bonner, 11, who founded the Little Red Wagon Foundation in 2005 to help homeless and underprivileged children, completed a 668-mile hike from Atlanta to Washington, DC, in July of 2009. Along the way, Zach collected thousands of letters from children to deliver to President Obama in the White House. On the final mile of his walk, Zach was joined by more than 500 supporters, including 300 kids who were homeless.

Zach raised more than $35,000 for this portion of the walk, as well as many other donations to support his cause, including 50 meals along the way from Cracker Barrel, 1,225 backpacks for homeless kids from Office Depot (for the number of miles he's walked in total), and an additional $25,000 donation from Elton John once he reached Washington, DC.

The previous two walks—from Tampa to Tallahassee in 2007 and from Tallahassee to Atlanta in 2008—raised about $42,000.

"These kids don't have a home; they don't have a safe place to sleep at night," he says. "They're out on the streets not because they want to be, but because it's out of their control."

The National Center on Family Homelessness estimates that 1.5 million children are homeless in the United States at some point each year. "It's getting worse . . . because of the depth of the economic recession and the staggering numbers of housing foreclosures nationally," President Ellen Bassuk says.

Zach's push to help other kids began after Hurricane Charley hit Florida in 2004. He went door to door with his red wagon to collect water, tarps, and other supplies. He collected 27 pickup-truck loads of supplies, he says. "To continue helping kids more efficiently," he and his mother established his foundation in 2005 (see the Web site littleredwagonfoundation.com).

THE FIFTY STATES

ALABAMA

Capital: Montgomery

Largest City: Birmingham

Became a State: December 14, 1819 (22nd)

Postal Code: AL

Population: 4,661,900

Area: 52,423 square miles

Nickname: Yellowhammer State

Motto: *Audemus jura nostra defendere* (We dare defend our rights)

Tree: Longleaf Pine

Flower: Camellia

Bird: Yellowhammer

Song: "Alabama"

Famous Folk: Harper Lee, Willie Mays, Rosa Parks

HAVE YOU HEARD?

Alabama workers built the first rocket that sent humans to the moon.

ALASKA

Capital: Juneau

Largest City: Anchorage

Became a State: January 3, 1959 (49th)

Postal Code: AK

Population: 686,293

Area: 656,425 square miles

Nickname: The Last Frontier

Motto: North to the Future

Tree: Sitka spruce

Flower: Forget Me Not

Bird: Willow Ptarmigan

Song: "Alaska's Flag"

Famous Folk: Jewel

HAVE YOU HEARD?

The official state sport of Alaska is dog mushing.

ARIZONA

Capital: Phoenix

Largest City: Phoenix

Became a State: February 14, 1912 (48th)

Postal Code: AZ

Population; 6,500,180

Area: 114,006 square miles

Nickname: Grand Canyon State

Motto: *Ditat Deus* (God enriches)

Tree: Yellow Paloverde

Flower: Saguaro Cactus Blossom

Bird: Cactus Wren

Songs: "Arizona"

Famous Folk: Geronimo, Linda Ronstadt, Kerri Strug

HAVE YOU HEARD?

Arizona is the nation's number one producer of copper, and the amount of copper on the roof of the Capitol building is equal to 4.8 million pennies.

ARKANSAS

Capital: Little Rock

Largest City: Little Rock

Became a State: June 15, 1836 (25th)

Postal Code: AR

Population: 2,855,390

Area: 53,182 square miles

Nickname: Natural State

Motto: *Regnat populus* (The people rule)

Tree: Loblolly Pine

Flower: Apple Blossom

Bird: Mockingbird

Song: "Arkansas"

Famous Folk: Johnny Cash, President Bill Clinton

HAVE YOU HEARD?

In 1985, milk was established as the official state beverage of Arkansas.

CALIFORNIA

Capital: Sacramento

Largest City: Los Angeles

Became a State: September 9, 1850 (31st)

Postal Code: CA

Population: 36,756,666

Area: 163,707 square miles

Nickname: Golden State

Motto: *Eureka* (I have found it)

Tree: Redwood

Flower: California Poppy

Bird: California Valley Quail

Song: "I Love You, California"

Famous Folk: Leonardo DiCaprio, Joe DiMaggio, Tiger Woods, John Steinbeck, President Richard Nixon

HAVE YOU HEARD?

There are more turkeys raised in California than in any other state in the Union.

COLORADO

Capital: Denver

Largest City: Denver

Became a State: August 1, 1867 (38th)

Postal Code: CO

Population: 4,939,456

Area: 104,100 square miles

Nicknames: Centennial State, Colorful Colorado

Motto: *Nil sine numine* (Nothing without providence)

Tree: Blue Spruce

Flower: Rocky Mountain Columbine

Bird: Lark Bunting

Song: "Where the Columbines Grow"

Famous Folk: Tim Allen

HAVE YOU HEARD?

Every May in Fruita, Colorado, there is a festival celebrating Mike the Headless Chicken. On September 10, 1945, farmer Lloyd Olsen chopped off the head of a rooster in preparation for his family's evening meal, and the rooster proceeded to live a healthy life for another 18 months with no head.

CONNECTICUT

Capital: Hartford

Largest City: Bridgeport

Became a State: January 9, 1788 (5th)

Postal Code: CT

Population: 3,501,252

Area: 5,544 square miles

Nickname: Constitution State

Motto: *Qui transtulit sustinet* (He who is transplanted still sustains)

Tree: White Oak

Flower: Mountain Laurel

Bird: Robin

Song: "Yankee Doodle"

Famous Folk: Katharine Hepburn, Nathan Hale, P. T. Barnum, President George W. Bush

HAVE YOU HEARD?

New Haven, Connecticut, is home to the very first lollipop-making machine, built in 1908.

ROBIN

DELAWARE

Capital: Dover

Largest City: Wilmington

Became a State: December 7, 1787 (1st)

Postal Code: DE

Population: 873,092

Area: 2,489 square miles

Nicknames: First State, Diamond State, Blue Hen State, Small Wonder

Motto: Liberty and Independence

Tree: American Holly

Flower: Peach Blossom

Bird: Blue Hen Chicken

Song: "Our Delaware"

Famous Folk: Valerie Bertinelli

HAVE YOU HEARD?

The ladybug is the Delaware state bug.

FLORIDA

Capital: Tallahassee

Largest City: Jacksonville

Became a State: March 3, 1845 (27th)

Postal Code: FL

Population: 18,328,340

Area: 65,758 square miles

Nickname: Sunshine State

Motto: In God We Trust

Tree: Cabbage Palmetto

Flower: Orange Blossom

Bird: Mockingbird

Song: "Swanee River"

Famous Folk: Fay Dunaway, Jim Morrison, Janet Reno

HAVE YOU HEARD?

Gatorade was created by scientists at the University of Florida and named after the school's football team, the Florida Gators.

GEORGIA

Capital: Atlanta

Largest City: Atlanta

Became a State: January 2, 1788 (4th)

Postal Code: GA

Population: 9,685,744

Area: 59,441 square miles

Nickname: Peach State

Motto: Wisdom, Justice, and Moderation

Tree: Live Oak

Flower: Cherokee Rose

Bird: Brown Thrasher

Song: "Georgia on My Mind"

Famous Folk: President Jimmy Carter, Ray Charles, Martin Luther King Jr., Hulk Hogan

HAVE YOU HEARD?

Coca-Cola was invented in 1885 by Dr. John Pemberton, a pharmacist in Columbus, Georgia, and first sold in May 1886, at Jacob's Pharmacy in Atlanta.

HAWAII

Capital: Honolulu

Largest City: Honolulu

Became a State: August 21, 1959 (50th)

Postal Code: HI

Population: 1,288,198

Area: 10,932 square miles

Nickname: Aloha State

Motto: *Ua mau ke ea o ka aina i ka pono* (The life of the land is perpetuated in righteousness)

Tree: Kukui (candlenut)

Flower: Hibiscus

Bird: Nene

Song: "*Hawai`i Pono`i* (Hawaii's Own)"

Famous Folk: President Barack Obama, Bette Midler, Lauren Graham

HAVE YOU HEARD?

Hawaii is the only state that grows coffee. Kona coffee is grown in the rich volcanic soil.

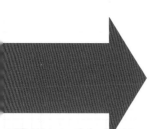

IDAHO

Capital: Boise

Largest City: Boise

Became a State: July 3, 1890 (43rd)

Postal Code: ID

Population: 1,523,816

Area: 83,574 square miles

Nickname: Gem State

Motto: *Esto perpetua* (Let it be perpetual)

Tree: Western White Pine

Flower: Syringa

Bird: Mountain Bluebird

Song: "Here We Have Idaho"

Famous Folk: Picabo Street, Ezra Pound, Lana Turner

HAVE YOU HEARD?

There is a law in Idaho forbidding its citizens from giving each other boxes of candy that weigh more than 50 pounds.

ILLINOIS

Capital: Springfield

Largest City: Chicago

Became a State: December 3, 1818 (21st)

Postal Code: IL

Population: 12,901,563

Area: 57,918 square miles

Nickname: Prairie State

Motto: State Sovereignty, National Union

Tree: White Oak

Flower: Purple Violet

Bird: Cardinal

Song: "Illinois"

Famous Folk: President Ronald Reagan, Michael Jordan, Harrison Ford, Oprah Winfrey, Ernest Hemingway

HAVE YOU HEARD?

The very first McDonald's was located in Des Plaines, Illinois.

INDIANA

Capital: Indianapolis

Largest City: Indianapolis

Became a State: December 11, 1816 (19th)

Postal Code: IN

Population: 6,376,792

Area: 36,420 square miles

Nickname: Hoosier State

Motto: The Crossroads of America

Tree: Yellow Poplar

Flower: Peony

Bird: Cardinal

Song: "On the Banks of the Wabash, Far Away"

Famous Folk: Michael Jackson, David Letterman, James Dean

HAVE YOU HEARD?

The town of Santa Claus, Indiana—the only official post office with this address—receives about half a million holiday cards and thousands of letters to Santa every year, from all over the world.

PEON

Idaho Potatoes

IOWA

Capital: Des Moines

Largest City: Des Moines

Became a State: December 28, 1846 (29th)

Postal Code: IA

Population: 3,002,555

Area: 56,276 square miles

Nickname: Hawkeye State

Motto: Our Liberties We Prize and Our Rights We Will Maintain

Tree: Oak

Flower: Wild Prairie Rose

Bird: Eastern Goldfinch

Song: "The Song of Iowa"

Famous Folk: President Herbert Hoover, Johnny Carson, John Wayne, Bill Bryson

HAVE YOU HEARD?

Strawberry Point, Iowa, boasts that it is home to the World's Largest Strawberry on a Stick—a bright red statue, 15 feet tall and made of fiberglass.

KANSAS

Capital: Topeka

Largest City: Wichita

Became a State: January 29, 1861 (34th)

Postal Code: KS

Population: 2,802,134

Area: 82,282 square miles

Nickname: Sunflower State

Motto: *Ad astra per aspera* (To the stars through difficulties)

Tree: Cottonwood

Flower: Sunflower

Bird: Western Meadowlark

Song: "Home on the Range"

Famous Folk: Amelia Earhart, Dennis Hopper, Eminem

HAVE YOU HEARD?

The windiest city in the United States is Dodge City, Kansas, with an average wind speed of 13.9 miles per hour.

KENTUCKY

Capital: Frankfurt

Largest City: Louisville

Became a State: June 1, 1792 (15th)

Postal Code: KY

Population: 4,269,245

Area: 40,411 square miles

Nickname: Bluegrass State

Motto: United We Stand, Divided We Fall

Tree: Yellow Poplar

Flower: Goldenrod

Bird: Cardinal

Song: "My Old Kentucky Home"

Famous Folk: President Abraham Lincoln, Muhammad Ali, Johnny Depp

HAVE YOU HEARD?

In 1893, two sisters from Louisville, Kentucky, composed the melody for what would become the song "Happy Birthday to You."

LOUISIANA

Capital: Baton Rouge

Largest City: New Orleans

Became a State: April 30, 1812 (18th)

Postal Code: LA

Population: 4,410,796

Area: 51,843 square miles

Nickname: Pelican State

Motto: Union, Justice, and Confidence

Tree: Bald Cypress

Flower: Magnolia

Bird: Eastern Brown Pelican

Song: "Give Me Louisiana"

Famous Folk: Louis Armstrong, Eli and Peyton Manning, Ellen Degeneres

HAVE YOU HEARD?

Instead of being divided into counties like most states, Louisiana is instead divided into 64 parishes (Alaska has boroughs).

MAINE

Capital: Augusta

Largest City: Portland

Became a State: March 15, 1820 (23rd)

Postal Code: ME

Population: 1,316,456

Area: 35,387 square miles

Nickname: Pine Tree State

Motto: *Dirigo* (I lead)

Tree: Eastern White Pine

Flower: White Pine Cone and Tassel

Bird: Chickadee

Song: "State Song of Maine"

Famous Folk: Stephen King, Patrick Dempsey, Leon Leonwood Bean (L. L. Bean)

HAVE YOU HEARD?

Maine is the only state with a one-syllable name.

MARYLAND

Capital: Annapolis

Largest City: Baltimore

Became a State: April 28, 1788 (7th)

Postal Code: MD

Population: 5,633,597

Area: 12,407 sq. miles

Nickname: Old Line State

Motto: *Fatti maschii parole femine* (manly deeds, womanly words)

Tree: White Oak

Flower: Black-eyed susan

Bird: Baltimore Oriole

Song: "Maryland, My Maryland"

Famous Folk: Babe Ruth, Harriet Tubman, David Hasselhoff

HAVE YOU HEARD?

In 1775, Mary Katherine Goddard became the postmaster of Baltimore, and became the first female in the colonies to hold a federal position.

MASSACHUSETTS

Capital: Boston

Largest City: Boston

Became a State: February 6, 1788 (6th)

Postal Code: MA

Population: 6,497,967

Area: 10,555 sq. miles

Nickname: Bay State

Motto: *Ense petit placidam sub libertate quietem* (By the sword we seek peace, but peace only under liberty)

Tree: American Elm

Flower: Mayflower

Bird: Chickadee

Song: All Hail to Massachusetts

Famous Folk: Presidents John Adams, John Quincy Adams, John F. Kennedy, and George H. W. Bush, Edgar Allen Poe, Dr. Suess, Leonard Nemoy

HAVE YOU HEARD?

In Rockport, Massachusetts, is a house made out of newspaper, begun in 1922 by Elis F. Stenman, a mechanical engineer. Even some of the furniture inside is made from varnished newspaper, including a piano.

MICHIGAN

Capital: Lansing

Largest City: Detroit

Became a State: January 26, 1837 (26th)

Postal Code: MI

Population: 10,003,422

Area: 96,810 sq. miles

Nickname: Wolverine State

Motto: *Si quaeris peninsulam amoenam, circumspice* (If you seek a pleasant peninsula, look about you)

Tree: Eastern white pine

Flower: Apple blossom

Bird: Robin

Song: "Michigan, My Michigan"

Famous Folk: Henry Ford, Serena Williams, Madonna

HAVE YOU HEARD?

Michigan is bordered by four of the five Great Lakes, and no matter where you stand in the state, you are never more than 85 miles away from one of them.

MINNESOTA

Capital: St. Paul

Largest City: Minneapolis

Became a State: May 11, 1858 (32nd)

Postal Code: MN

Population: 5,220,393

Area: 86,943 sq. miles

Nickname: North Star State

Motto: *L'Etoile du nord* (The star of the north)

Tree: Red pine

Flower: Pink-and-white lady slipper

Bird: Common loon

Song: "Hail! Minnesota"

Famous Folk: John Madden, Bob Dylan, Jessica Biel

HAVE YOU HEARD?

The Mall of America in Bloomington, Minnesota—the largest mall in the country in terms of floor space—has a gross building area of 4.2 million square feet, 12,550 parking spaces, and 11,000 year-round employees.

MISSISSIPPI

Capital: Jackson

Largest City: Jackson

Became a State: December 10, 1817 (20th)

Postal Code: MS

Population: 2,938,618

Area: 48,434 sq. miles

Nickname: Magnolia State

Motto: *Virtute et armis* (By valor and arms)

Tree: Southern Magnolia

Flower: Magnolia

Bird: Mockingbird

Song: "Go, Mississippi"

Famous Folk: William Faulkner, Elvis Presley, Brett Favre, Oprah Winfrey

HAVE YOU HEARD?

The world's largest cactus plantation is in Edwards, Mississippi.

MOCK-ING-BIRD

MISSOURI

Capital: Jefferson City

Largest City: Kansas City

Became a State: August 10, 1821 (24th)

Postal Code: MO

Population: 5,911,605

Area: 69,709 sq. miles

Nickname: Show Me State

Motto: *Salus populi suprema lex esto* (The welfare of the people shall be the supreme law)

Tree: Flowering Dogwood

Flower: Hawthorn

Bird: Bluebird

Song: "Missouri Waltz"

Famous Folk: President Harry S Truman, Mark Twain, Maya Angelou, Sheryl Crow

HAVE YOU HEARD?

Legend has it that Missouri's nickname as the Show Me State began when U.S. Congressman Willard Duncan Vandiver gave a speech at a naval banquet in 1899 asserting that "frothy eloquence" would never convince him of anything: "I am from Missouri," he declared. "You have got to show me."

MONTANA

Capital: Helena

Largest City: Billings

Became a State: November 8, 1889 (41st)

Postal Code: MT

Population: 967,440

Area: 147,046 sq. miles

Nickname: Treasure State

Motto: *Oro y plata* (Gold and silver)

Tree: Ponderosa Pine

Flower: Bitterroot

Bird: Western meadowlark

Song: "Montana"

Famous Folk: Evel Knievel, Michelle Williams

HAVE YOU HEARD?

The population of elk, deer, and antelope in Montana outnumber the humans there.

NEBRASKA

Capital: Lincoln

Largest City: Omaha

Became a State: March 1, 1867 (37th)

Postal Code: NE

Population: 1,783,432

Area: 77,358 sq. miles

Nickname: Cornhusker State

Motto: Equality before the law

Tree: Cottonwood

Flower: Goldenrod

Bird: Western meadowlark

Song: "Beautiful Nebraska"

Famous Folk: President Gerald Ford, Marlon Brando, Andy Roddick

HAVE YOU HEARD?

In 1910, an ordinance was created in Waterloo, Nebraska, prohibiting barbers from eating onions during the day.

NEVADA

Capital: Carson City

Largest City: Las Vegas

Became a State: October 31, 1864 (36th)

Postal Code: NV

Population: 2,600,167

Area: 110,567 sq. miles

Nickname: The Silver State

Motto: All for our country

Tree: Bristlecone pine

Flower: Sagebrush

Bird: Mountain bluebird

Song: "Home Means Nevada"

Famous Folk: Andre Agassi, Pat Nixon

HAVE YOU HEARD?

The Hoover Dam, built with sides in both Nevada and Arizona to improve the flow of the Colorado River, is made of 3.25 million cubic yards of concrete—enough to pave a roadway from California to New York.

NEW HAMPSHIRE

Capital: Concord

Largest City: Manchester

Became a State: June 21, 1788 (9th)

Postal Code: NH

Population: 1,315,809

Area: 9,351 sq. miles

Nickname: Granite State

Motto: Live free or die

Tree: Paper birch

Flower: Purple lilac

Bird: Purple finch

Song: "Old New Hampshire"

Famous Folk: Dan Brown, Mandy Moore, Sarah Silverman

HAVE YOU HEARD?

New Hampshire was the first state to declare its independence from England and adopt its own state constitution, six months before the actual signing of the Declaration of Independence.

NEW JERSEY

Capital: Trenton

Largest City: Newark

Became a State: December 18, 1787 (3rd)

Postal Code: NJ

Population: 8,682,661

Area: 8,722 sq. miles

Nickname: Garden State

Motto: Liberty and Prosperity

Tree: Northern red oak

Flower: Violet

Bird: Eastern goldfinch

Song: "I'm From New Jersey"

Famous Folk: Grover Cleveland, Derek Jeter, Bruce Springsteen, The Jonas Brothers, Meryl Streep

HAVE YOU HEARD?

New Jersey has more diners than any other state, and is sometimes actually referred to as "the diner capital of the world."

NEW MEXICO

Capital: Sante Fe

Largest City: Albuquerque

Became a State: January 6, 1912 (47th)

Postal Code: NM

Population: 1,984,356

Area: 121,593 sq. miles

Nickname: Land of Enchantment

Motto: *Crescit eundo* (It grows as it goes)

Tree: Pinyon pine

Flower: Yucca flower

Bird: Roadrunner

Song: "O, Fair New Mexico"

Famous Folk: Jeff Bezos, Demi Moore, Neil Patrick Harris

HAVE YOU HEARD?

At 7,000 feet above sea level, Sante Fe is the highest capital city in the United States.

NEW YORK

Capital: Albany

Largest City: New York

Became a State: July 26, 1788 (11th)

Postal Code: NY

Population: 19,490,297

Area: 54,475 sq. miles

Nickname: Empire State

Motto: *Excelsior* (Excellence)

Tree: Sugar maple

Flower: Rose

Bird: Bluebird

Song: "I Love New York"

Famous Folk: Woody Allen, Anne Hathaway, Herman Melville, Humphrey Bogart, Tom Cruise, Jimmy Fallon, Timothy Geithner, Jay-Z

HAVE YOU HEARD?

First established in 1803 by Alexander Hamilton, the *New York Post* is the oldest running newspaper in the United States.

Lady Liberty

NORTH CAROLINA

Capital: Raleigh

Largest City: Charlotte

Became a State: November 21, 1789 (12th)

Postal Code: NC

Population: 9,222,414

Area: 53,821 sq. miles

Nickname: Old North State

Motto: *Esse quam videri* (To be, rather than to seem)

Tree: Longleaf pine

Flower: Dogwood

Bird: Cardinal

Song: "The Old North State"

Famous Folk: Clay Aiken, Jaime Pressly, Dale Earnhardt

HAVE YOU HEARD?

On December 17, 1903, Wilbur and Orville Wright completed the first successful airplane flight in Kitty Hawk, North Carolina, an achievement that is commemorated by the Wright Memorial at Kitty Hawk.

Cardinal

NORTH DAKOTA

Capital: Bismarck

Largest City: Fargo

Became a State: November 2, 1889 (39th)

Postal Code: ND

Population: 641,481

Area: 70,704 sq. miles

Nickname: Peace Garden State

Motto: Liberty and union, now and forever, one and inseparable

Tree: American elm

Flower: Wild prairie rose

Bird: Western meadowlark

Song: "North Dakota Hymn"

Famous Folk: Louis L'Amour, Phil Jackson, Lawrence Welk

HAVE YOU HEARD?

The town of Rugby, North Dakota, is known as the geographic center of North America; this honor is marked with a 15-foot high rock obelisk and flag poles flying the U.S. and Canadian flags.

OHIO

Capital: Columbus

Largest City: Columbus

Became a State: March 1, 1803 (17th)

Postal Code: OH

Population: 11,485,910

Area: 44,828 sq. miles

Nickname: Buckeye State

Motto: With God, all things are possible

Tree: Ohio buckeye

Flower: Scarlet carnation

Bird: Cardinal

Song: "Beautiful Ohio"

Famous Folk: Paul Newman, Thomas Edison, Sarah Jessica Parker, LeBron James

HAVE YOU HEARD?

In 1879, a saloon keeper in Dayton, Ohio, named James Ritty invented the first cash register to protect his profits from sticky-fingered employees.

CARNATION

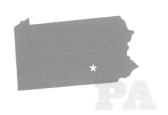

OKLAHOMA

Capital: Oklahoma City

Largest City: Oklahoma City

Became a State: November 16, 1907 (46th)

Postal Code: OK

Population: 3,642,361

Area: 69,903 sq. miles

Nickname: Sooner State

Motto: *Labor omnia vincit* (Labor conquers all things)

Tree: Redbud

Flower: Mistletoe

Bird: Scissor-tailed flycatcher

Song: "Oklahoma"

Famous Folk: Brad Pitt, Carrie Underwood, Mickey Mantle

HAVE YOU HEARD?

The town of Beaver, Oklahoma, holds the annual World Championship Cow Chip Throw, and is known as the cow chip throwing capital of the world. Cow chips—or dried cow dung—are affectionately called the Frisbees of the prairie.

MISTLETOE

OREGON

Capital: Salem

Largest City: Portland

Became a State: February 14, 1859 (33rd)

Postal Code: OR

Population: 3,790,060

Area: 98,386 sq. miles

Nickname: Beaver State

Motto: *Alis Volat Propiis* (She Flies With Her Own Wings)

Tree: Douglas fir

Flower: Oregon grape

Bird: Western meadowlark

Song: "Oregon, My Oregon"

Famous Folk: Raymond Carver, Brian Walker, Matt Groening

HAVE YOU HEARD?

Oregon's Crater Lake, formed in the remains of the ancient volcano Mount Mazama, is the deepest lake in the United States.

PENNSYLVANIA

Capital: Harrisburg

Largest City: Philadelphia

Became a State: December 12, 1787 (2nd)

Postal Code: PA

Population: 12,448,279

Area: 46,058 sq. miles

Nickname: Keystone State

Motto: Virtue, Liberty, and Independence

Tree: Eastern hemlock

Flower: Mountain laurel

Bird: Ruffed grouse

Song: "Pennsylvania"

Famous Folk: Kevin Bacon, Joseph Biden, Tina Fey, Joe Namath, Taylor Swift

HAVE YOU HEARD?

Forbes Field, the very first baseball stadium, was built in 1909 in Pittsburgh, Pennsylvania.

JOE BIDE

RHODE ISLAND

Capital: Providence

Largest City: Providence

Became a State: May 29, 1790 (13th)

Postal Code: RI

Population: 1,050,788

Area: 1,545 sq. miles

Nickname: The Ocean State

Motto: Hope

Tree: Red maple

Flower: Violet

Bird: Rhode Island red

Song: "Rhode Island's It For Me"

Famous Folk: Meredith Vieira, Cormac McCarthy,

HAVE YOU HEARD?

At an area of 1,545 square miles, Rhode Island is geographically the smallest state in the United States.

SOUTH CAROLINA

Capital: Columbia

Largest City: Columbia

Became a State: May 23, 1788 (8th)

Postal Code: SC

Population: 4,479,800

Area: 32,007 sq. miles

Nickname: Palmetto State

Motto: *Animis Opibusque Parati / Dum Spiro Spero* (Prepared in mind and resources / While I breathe, I hope)

Tree: Cabbage palmetto

Flower: Yellow jessamine

Bird: Great Carolina wren

Song: "Carolina"

Famous Folk: President Andrew Jackson, Mary-Louise Parker, Chris Rock

HAVE YOU HEARD?

The official state dance of South Carolina is a rhythm and blues number called the "Carolina Shag."

SOUTH DAKOTA

Capital: Pierre

Largest City: Sioux Falls

Became a State: November 2, 1889 (40th)

Postal Code: SD

Population: 804,194

Area: 77,121 sq. miles

Nickname: Mount Rushmore State

Motto: Under God the people rule

Tree: White spruce

Flower: Pasque flower

Bird: Ring-necked pheasant

Song: "Hail, South Dakota"

Famous Folk: Tom Daschle, Tom Brokaw, Crazy Horse

HAVE YOU HEARD?

Mount Rushmore, South Dakota's massive granite sculpture that commemorates the first 150 years of United States history with carved images of George Washington, Thomas Jefferson, Theodore Roosevelt and Abraham Lincoln, covers nearly 1,300 acres and took 400 people 14 years to complete.

TENNESSEE

Capital: Nashville

Largest City: Memphis

Became a State: June 1, 1796 (16th)

Postal Code: TN

Population: 6,214,888

Area: 42,146 sq. miles

Nickname: Volunteer State

Motto: Agriculture and Commerce

Tree: Yellow poplar

Flower: Iris

Bird: Mockingbird

Song: "Tennessee"

Famous Folk: Albert Gore Jr., Aretha Franklin, Justin Timberlake, Miley Cyrus

HAVE YOU HEARD?

The Copper Basin, a more than fifty-square-mile scorched desert near Ducktown, Tennessee, was in such stark contrast from the lush surrounding areas that it could be seen by astronauts from space. The land, environmentally decimated by nineteenth-century mining practices, has since become the focus of a dedicated reclamation and reforestation project.

TEXAS

Capital: Austin

Largest City: Houston

Became a State: December 29, 1845 (28th)

Postal Code: TX

Population: 24,326,974

Area: 268,601 sq. miles

Nickname: Lone Star State

Motto: Friendship

Tree: Pecan

Flower: Bluebonnet

Bird: Mockingbird

Song: "Texas, Our Texas"

Famous Folk: Presidents Dwight D. Eisenhower, and Lyndon B. Johnson, Lance Armstrong, Beyoncé Knowles

HAVE YOU HEARD?

Texas produces more wool than any other state in the country.

UTAH

Capital: Salt Lake City

Largest City: Salt Lake City

Became a State: January 4, 1896 (45th)

Postal Code: UT

Population: 2,736,424

Area: 84,904 sq. miles

Nickname: The Beehive State

Motto: Industry

Tree: Blue spruce

Flower: Sego lily

Bird: California gull

Song: "Utah, We Love Thee"

Famous Folk: Butch Cassidy, Marie Osmond

HAVE YOU HEARD?

Due to its location so far inland, the snow in Utah is unusually dry, giving it the reputation of having the world's greatest powder. With its tall mountain peaks and generous helpings of this great snow, it hosts many popular alpine ski resorts.

VERMONT

Capital: Montpelier

Largest City: Burlington

Became a State: March 4, 1791 (14th)

Postal Code: VT

Population: 621,270

AreaL 9,615 sq. miles

Nickname: Green Mountain State

Motto: Freedom and unity

Tree: Sugar maple

Flower: Red clover

Bird: Hermit thrush

Song: "These Green Mountains"

Famous Folk: Presidents Chester A. Arthur, and Calvin Coolidge

HAVE YOU HEARD?

Montpelier, Vermont, is, by population, the smallest state capital in the United States, as well as the only one without a McDonald's.

VIRGINIA

Capital: Richmond

Largest City: Virginia Beach

Became a State: June 25, 1788 (10th)

Postal Code: VA

Population: 7,769,089

Area: 42,769 sq. miles

Nickname: Old Dominion State

Motto: *Sic Semper Tyrannis* (Thus Always to Tyrants)

Tree: Flowering dogwood

Flower: Dogwood

Bird: Cardinal

Song: "Carry Me Back to Old Virginia"

Famous Folk: Presidents George Washington, Thomas Jefferson, James Madison, James Monroe, William Henry Harrison, John Tyler, Zachary Taylor, and Woodrow Wilson, Sandra Bullock, Katie Couric, Pocahontis

HAVE YOU HEARD?

Virginia was named for Queen Elizabeth I of England, the "Virgin Queen."

WASHINGTON

Capital: Olympia

Largest City: Seattle

Became a State: November 11, 1889 (42nd)

Postal Code: WA

Population: 6,549,224

Area: 71,303 sq. miles

Nickname: The Evergreen State

Motto: *Alki* (Bye and Bye)

Tree: Western hemlock

Flower: Pink rhododendron

Bird: Willow goldfinch

Song: "Washington, My Home"

Famous Folk: Hillary Swank, Bill Gates, Jimi Hendrix

HAVE YOU HEARD?

Washington is the only state named after a U.S. president.

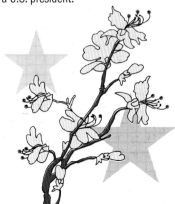

WEST VIRGINIA
Capital: Charleston

Largest City: Charleston

Became a State: June 20, 1863 (35th)

Postal Code: WV

Population: 1,814,468

Area: 24,231 sq. miles

Nickname: Mountain State

Motto: *Montani semper liberi* (Mountaineers are always free)

Tree: Sugar maple

Flower: Rhododendron

Bird: Cardinal

Song: "The West Virginia Hills"

Famous Folk: Mary Lou Retton, Brad Paisley, Pearl Buck

HAVE YOU HEARD?

Mother's Day was first celebrated in the United States on May 10, 1908, at the Andrews Methodist Church in Grafton, West Virginia.

WISCONSIN
Capital: Madison

Largest City: Milwaukee

Became a State: May 29, 1848 (30th)

Postal Code: WI

Population: 5,627,967

Area: 65,503 sq. miles

Nickname: Badger State

Motto: Forword

Tree: Sugar maple

Flower: Wood violet

Bird: Robin

Song: "On Wisconsin"

Famous Folk: Danica Patrick, Georgia O'Keeffe, Chris Noth, Laura Ingalls Wilder

HAVE YOU HEARD?

Wisconsin is called the Badger State to honor not the actual badger (the state animal), but the state's early settlers: miners in the 1800s who searched for lead by digging tunnels in the Wisconsin earth and then lived in them during the cold winter months.

WYOMING
Capital: Cheyenne

Largest City: Cheyenne

Became a State: July 10, 1890 (44th)

Postal Code: WY

Population: 532,668

Area: 97,818 sq. miles

Nickname: Equality State

Motto: Equal rights

Tree: Cottonwood

Flower: Indian paintbrush

Bird: Western meadowlark

Song: "Wyoming"

Famous Folk: Jackson Pollock, Matthew Fox

HAVE YOU HEARD?

Wyoming was the first state to give women the right to vote, in 1869 (at the time, it was called the Wyoming Territories); when Wyoming was officially admitted into the Union in 1890, women's suffrage was included in their constitution.

WASHINGTON, D.C.
(The District of Columbia)

On December 1, 1800, Washington, D.C. became the capital of the United States.

Population: 591,833

Area: 68 sq. miles

Motto: *Justitia Omnibus* (Justice to all)

Tree: Scarlet oak

Flower: American beauty rose

Bird: Wood thrush

Song: "The Star-Spangled Banner"

Famous Folk: John F. Kennedy Jr., Al Gore, Stephen Colbert, Pete Sampras, Katherine Heigl

HAVE YOU HEARD?

The famous red emergency phone that is often seen in movies is not actually located in the Oval Office, but in the Pentagon.

PUERTO RICO AND OTHER U.S. TERRITORIES

Capital: San Juan

Largest City: San Juan

Population: 3,954,037

Area (land): 3,459 sq. miles

Nickname: *Isla del Encanto* (Isle of Enchantment)

Motto: *Johannes est nomen eius* (*Juan es su nombre*, John is his name)

Tree: Ceiba (silk-cotton tree)

Flower: Maga (Puerto Rican hibiscus)

Bird: Reinita (stripe-headed tanager)

Song: "The Borinquen Anthem"

Famous Folk: Jorge Posada

HAVE YOU HEARD?

Baseball is the national sport of Puerto Rico.

U.S. GOVERNMENT ORGANIZATION

"We the People of the United States, in Order to form a more perfect Union, establish Justice, ensure domestic Tranquility, provide for the common defense, promote the general Welfare, and secure the Blessings of Liberty to ourselves and our Posterity, do ordain and establish this Constitution for the United States of America."

—THE PREAMBLE TO THE CONSTITUTION

The U.S. Constitution

The Constitution, written in 1787 and put into effect in 1789, remains to this day the supreme law of the United States. Supported by the legislature of the states, the constitution is the source of all governmental power, while simultaneously protecting the rights of the people, by whom and for whom it was written, by placing key restrictions on the government and the way it may exercise this power. An important system of checks and balances was created by dividing the power of the government into three separate branches: the executive (led by the president), the legislative (Congress) and the judicial (the Supreme Court and other federal courts). Special attention was also paid to clearly defining the relationship between the states and to establishing a strict and egalitarian process that must be followed to make any amendments, of which there have been twenty-seven (although one banning the manufacture and sale of liquor has since been repealed).

We THE PeOPLe...

The Bill of Rights

The Bill of Rights, the first ten amendments to the Constitution that were passed together in 1791, presents a clear catalog of the basic civil liberties that are still considered fundamental to American life.

The First Amendment guarantees the rights of freedom of religion, speech, assembly, and the press.

The Second Amendment gives citizens the right to bear arms.

The Third Amendment prohibits the government from lodging troops in private homes without the owner's consent (this was a problem for many people during the American Revolution).

The Fourth Amendment protects people, their homes, and their belongings from being searched without reasonable cause and legal consent.

The Fifth Amendment protects the rights of all people on trial for crimes, guaranteeing them due process of the law.

The Sixth Amendment guarantees the right of all citizens accused of crimes to a speedy public trial by jury and to legal representation.

The Seventh Amendment guarantees that civil cases also be tried by jury.

The Eighth Amendment guarantees that reasonable amounts be set for fines and bail and prohibits cruel and unusual punishments.

The Ninth Amendment states that the list of rights enumerated in the Constitution is not exhaustive and that the people retain many other rights not enumerated.

The Tenth Amendment establishes that all powers not delegated to the federal government belong to either the states or the people.

The Judicial Branch

The primary responsibility of the judicial branch is to uphold the U.S. Constitution and all of its laws. The judicial branch is composed of nine justices of the **Supreme Court** and numerous federal judges, and all are appointed by the president and approved by the Senate. The Supreme Court is the highest court in the U.S. court system. The chief justice, one of the nine, leads all Court meetings, and all decisions are made by a majority vote. The Supreme Court is tasked with judging cases pertaining to federal laws, disputes between states, actions of the president, and all interpretations and potential violations of the Constitution. The Supreme Court is the final stop for any case that goes that far, most of which have been tried in other state or federal courts before they come before the Supreme Court.

Judica

The Executive Branch

The executive branch of the federal government is led by the president, who is elected into office by the people every four years, for no more than two terms. The president is commander-in-chief of the U.S. armed forces and is responsible for enforcing the laws written by Congress and appointing all heads of federal agencies, including the cabinet. The cabinet is in charge of the day-to-day administration of federal laws and includes the vice president and many members called secretaries, the heads of major executive departments. When you include the members of the armed forces, the executive branch includes more than four million employees.

THE 15 DEPARTMENTS OF THE CABINET:

AGRICULTURE	INTERIOR
COMMERCE	JUSTICE
DEFENSE	LABOR
EDUCATION	STATE
ENERGY	TRANSPORTATION
HEALTH AND HUMAN SERVICES	TREASURY
HOMELAND SECURITY	VETERANS AFFAIRS
HOUSING AND URBAN DEVELOPMENT	

The Legislative Branch

The legislative branch of the U.S. government is the two chambers of the Congress: the Senate and the House of Representatives.

The **Senate** always contains 100 members, two from each state, regardless of its size. The Constitution holds that each and every state must have equal representation in the Senate, so this number never wavers. Senators are elected to six-year terms, with no limit on the number of terms they can serve. The vice president leads all sessions of the Senate, in which he or she has the power to ratify all treaties made by the president, approve or reject high-level presidential appointments, and conduct trials of federal officials impeached by the House of Representatives.

The **House of Representatives** is made up of 435 members (a number that has been held since 1911), with a certain number of seats allotted to each state according to its population. Every state must have at least one representative, and the more people who live in each state, the more representatives it has. Representatives are elected to two-year terms, with no limit to the number of terms they can serve. The Speaker of the House leads all sessions of the House of Representatives, in which he or she has the power to create revenue-related bills that enable the government to make and spend money, vote to impeach elected officials, and elect the president in the case of an electoral college deadlock.

PRESIDENTS

GEORGE WASHINGTON Federalist Party 1789–97
Vice president: John Adams **First lady:** Martha Dandridge Custis
Born: February 22, 1732, Virginia **Died:** December 14, 1799
Have You Heard? On July 9, 1776, General George Washington had the Declaration of Independence read out loud to his army.

JOHN ADAMS Federalist Party 1797–1801
Vice president: Thomas Jefferson **First lady:** Abigail Smith
Born: October 30, 1735, Massachusetts **Died:** July 4, 1826
Have You Heard? On John Adams's second night spent in the new White House (which was built between 1792 and 1800), he wrote in a letter to his wife: "I pray to Heaven to bestow the best of Blessings on this house and all that shall hereafter inhabit it. May none but honest and wise Men ever rule under this roof."

THOMAS JEFFERSON Democratic-Republican Party 1801–09
Vice presidents: Aaron Burr, George Clinton **First lady:** Martha Wayles Skelton
Born: April 13, 1743, Virginia **Died:** July 4, 1826
Have You Heard? Thomas Jefferson, a lifelong fan of classical architecture, spent more than 40 years designing and building Monticello, his home in Charlottesville, Virginia.

JAMES MADISON Democratic-Republican Party 1809–17
Vice presidents: George Clinton, Elbridge Gerry **First lady:** Dolley Payne Todd
Born: March 16, 1751, Virginia **Died:** June 28, 1836
Have You Heard? James Madison was younger than both of his vice presidents, who both died while in office.

JAMES MONROE Democratic-Republican Party 1817–25
Vice president: Daniel D. Tompkins **First lady:** Elizabeth Kortright
Born: April 28, 1758, Virginia **Died:** July 4, 1831
Have You Heard? The capital of Liberia, originally called Christopolis, was renamed Monrovia after James Monroe. Liberia was founded by Americans to give freed slaves a place to return to in Africa.

JOHN QUINCY ADAMS Democratic-Republican Party 1825–29
Vice president: John C. Calhoun **First lady:** Louisa Catherine Johnson
Born: July 11, 1767, Massachusetts **Died:** February 23, 1848
Have You Heard? John Quincy Adams was a president with quirky personal habits: he had a pet alligator (which he kept in the East Wing); he had the first pool table installed in the White House; and he liked to begin his days with a nude swim in the Potomac River.

ANDREW JACKSON Democratic Party 1829–37
Vice presidents: John C. Calhoun, Martin Van Buren **First lady:** Rachel Donelson Robards
Born: March 15, 1767, South Carolina **Died:** June 8, 1845
Have You Heard? Andrew Jackson had a pet parrot named Pol who was taught to curse in English and Spanish; legend has it that Pol had to be removed from Jackson's funeral service when it let loose with some loud profanity.

MARTIN VAN BUREN Democratic Party 1837–41
Vice president: Richard M. Johnson **First lady:** Hannah Hoes
Born: December 5, 1782, New York **Died:** July 24, 1862
Have You Heard? The term "O.K." originated during Martin Van Buren's presidential campaign. Clubs created in support of his campaign were called O.K. Clubs, and the expression eventually came to mean "all right."

WILLIAM H. HARRISON Whig Party 1841
Vice president: John Tyler **First lady:** Anna Symmes
Born: February 9, 1773, Virginia **Died:** April 4, 1841
Have You Heard? William Henry Harrison was the first president who also studied medicine; unfortunately, he was also the first president to die in office, just thirty-one days in.

JOHN TYLER Whig Party 1841–45
Vice president: None **First ladies:** Letitia Christian (d. 1842), Julia Gardiner
Born: March 29, 1790, Virginia **Died:** January 18, 1862
Have You Heard? Twenty years after his term, John Tyler—sometimes called "His Accidency," as he was the first person named to the presidency without being elected to it—joined the Confederacy at the beginning of the Civil War and became the only president to find himself a sworn enemy of the United States.

JAMES K. POLK Democratic Party 1845–49
Vice president: George M. Dallas **First lady:** Sarah Childress
Born: November 2, 1795, North Carolina **Died:** June 15, 1849
Have You Heard? James Polk spent only thirty-seven days away from his desk during the entire four years of his term. He was also the first president to voluntarily retire after one term: he vowed to serve only one term and stuck to his promise.

ZACHARY TAYLOR Whig Party 1849–50
Vice president: Millard Fillmore **First lady:** Margaret Smith
Born: November 24, 1784, Virginia **Died:** July 9, 1850
Have You Heard? As a soldier who was always on the move, Zachary Taylor wasn't able to establish a legal residency until he after he retired; because of this, he wasn't able to vote until age sixty-two, including in his own election.

MILLARD FILLMORE Whig Party 1850–53
Vice president: none **First ladies:** Abigail Powers (d. 1853), Caroline Carmichael McIntosh
Born: January 7, 1800, New York **Died:** March 8, 1874
Have You Heard? Two years after his presidency, while traveling in Europe, Millard Fillmore was offered an honorary Doctor of Civil Law degree but declined the honor, saying that he had neither "the literary nor scientific attainment" and that "no man should accept a degree he cannot read."

FRANKLIN PIERCE Democratic Party 1853–57
Vice president: William R. King **First lady:** Jane Means Appleton
Born: November 23, 1804, New Hampshire **Died:** October 8, 1869
Have You Heard? One of the party slogans of the Democrats when Pierce ran for office was "We Polked you in 1844; we shall Pierce you in 1852."

JAMES BUCHANAN Democratic Party 1857–61
Vice president: John C. Breckinridge **First lady:** none
Born: April 23, 1791, Pennsylvania **Died:** June 1, 1868
Have You Heard? James Buchanan is the only president to never marry and is said to have had the neatest handwriting of any president.

ABRAHAM LINCOLN Republican Party 1861–65
Vice presidents: Hannibal Hamlin, Andrew Johnson **First lady:** Mary Todd
Born: February 12, 1809, Kentucky **Died:** April 15, 1865
Have You Heard? Abraham Lincoln loved the writing of Edgar Allen Poe and shared with his wife a passion for psychic phenomena—in fact, the two of them held séances at the White House.

ANDREW JOHNSON Democratic Party 1865–69
Vice president: none **First lady:** Eliza McCardle
Born: December 29, 1808, North Carolina **Died:** July 31, 1875
Have You Heard? Andrew Johnson was the only president who was also a skilled (and self-taught) tailor—he made his own clothes, as well as some for members of his cabinet.

ULYSSES S. GRANT Republican Party 1869–77
Vice presidents: Schuyler Colfax, Henry Wilson **First lady:** Julia Dent
Born: April 27, 1822, Ohio **Died:** July 23, 1885
Have You Heard? Ulysses S. Grant was a light smoker until a reporter once saw him holding a cigar and wrote about it; thereafter, many thousands of cigars were sent to him as gifts and his habit drastically increased. He died of throat cancer.

RUTHERFORD B. HAYES Republican Party 1877–81
Vice president: William A. Wheeler **First lady:** Lucy Ware Webb
Born: October 4, 1822, Ohio **Died:** January 17, 1893
Have You Heard? Rutherford B. Hayes and his wife hosted the first Easter egg roll on the White House lawn, a tradition that continues today.

JAMES A. GARFIELD Republican Party 1881
Vice president: Chester A. Arthur **First lady:** Lucretia Rudolph
Born: November 19, 1831, Ohio **Died:** September 19, 1881
Have You Heard? James Garfield was the first left-handed president and is the only president who was also a preacher.

CHESTER A. ARTHUR Republican Party 1881–85
Vice president: none **First lady:** Ellen Lewis Herndon
Born: October 5, 1829, Vermont **Died:** November 18, 1886
Have You Heard? Chester Arthur was known for his elegant style of dress; he changed his pants several times a day and is said to have owned more than eighty pairs.

GROVER CLEVELAND Democratic Party 1885–89
Vice president: Thomas A. Hendricks **First lady:** Frances Folsom
Born: March 18, 1837, New Jersey **Died:** June 24, 1908
Have You Heard? During the painful economic crisis of 1893, Grover Cleveland learned of a cancerous grown in his mouth; so as not to create panic, he snuck off on a boat with his doctors to have it removed, telling the public he was simply on a fishing trip.

BENJAMIN HARRISON Republican Party 1889–93
Vice president: Levi P. Morton **First ladies:** Caroline Lavinia Scott (d. 1892), Mary Scott Lord Dimmick
Born: August 20, 1833, Ohio **Died:** March 13, 1901
Have You Heard? Benjamin Harrison was the first president to use electricity in the White House, although his family never became comfortable with it, and his wife was too nervous to touch the switches at all.

GROVER CLEVELAND Democratic Party 1893–97
Vice president: Adlai E. Stevenson **First lady:** Frances Folsom
Born: March 18, 1837, New Jersey **Died:** June 24, 1908
Have You Heard? Grover Cleveland was the only president to be elected to the office for two nonconsecutive terms.

WILLIAM MCKINLEY Republican Party 1897–1901
Vice presidents: Garret A. Hobart, Theodore Roosevelt **First lady:** Ida Saxton
Born: January 29, 1843, Ohio **Died:** September 14, 1901
Have You Heard? Shortly after he was shot twice—with bullets that eight days later would result in his death—William McKinley, watching as his shooter was tackled and beaten, cried out: "Don't let them hurt him!"

THEODORE ROOSEVELT Republican Party 1901–09
Vice president: Charles W. Fairbanks **First lady:** Edith Kermit Carow
Born: October 27, 1858, New York **Died:** January 6, 1919
Have You Heard? On a Mississippi hunting expedition during Theodore Roosevelt's presidency, a few fellow hunter got a small black bear caught in a tree and then called him over to take the shot. However, Roosevelt decided not to shoot the trapped little bear. A New York toymaker caught wind of the story and named a stuffed bear the Teddy Bear in his honor.

WILLIAM H. TAFT Republican Party 1909–13
Vice president: James S. Sherman **First lady:** Helen Herron
Born: September 15, 1857, Ohio **Died:** March 8, 1930
Have You Heard? William Taft is the only president who also served as chief justice of the United States.

WOODROW WILSON Democratic Party 1913–21
Vice president: Thomas R. Marshall **First ladies:** Ellen Louise Axson (d. 1914), Edith Bolling Galt
Born: December 28, 1856, Virginia **Died:** February 3, 1924
Have You Heard? In 1915, Woodrow Wilson was the first president to attend a World Series game: he went with his new fiancée, Edith Galt, and insisted on paying for their tickets.

WARREN G. HARDING Republican Party 1921–23
Vice president: Calvin Coolidge **First lady:** Florence Kling
Born: November 2, 1865, Ohio **Died:** August 2, 1923
Have You Heard? Warren Harding was the first president to speak on the radio and, in fact, the first president to have a radio.

CALVIN COOLIDGE Republican Party 1923–29
Vice president: Charles G. Dawes **First lady:** Grace Anna Goodhue
Born: July 4, 1872, Vermont **Died:** January 5, 1933
Have You Heard? Calvin Coolidge was a man of so few words that once a young woman attending a dinner party at which he would also be made a bet that she could get him to say more than two words to her that evening. When she sat next to him and told him of the bet she had made, he quietly replied: "You lose."

HERBERT HOOVER Republican Party 1929–33
Vice president: Charles Curtis **First lady:** Lou Henry
Born: August 10, 1874, Iowa **Died:** October 20, 1964
Have You Heard? Both Herbert Hoover and his wife Lou spoke fluent Chinese, which they often lapsed into when they didn't want others around them to know what they were talking about.

FRANKLIN D. ROOSEVELT Democratic Party 1933–45
Vice presidents: John Garner, Henry Wallace, Harry S Truman
First lady: Anna Eleanor Roosevelt
Born: January 30, 1882, New York **Died:** April 12, 1945
Have You Heard? Franklin Roosevelt was the first president ever to appear on television, and although he died in office, he held the presidency for twelve years, longer than any other president. The limit is now two terms, or eight years.

HARRY S TRUMAN Democratic Party 1945–53
Vice president: Alben W. Barkley **First lady:** Elizabeth Virginia "Bess" Wallace
Born: May 8, 1884, Missouri **Died:** December 26, 1972
Have You Heard? Harry Truman's middle initial S doesn't stand for one particular name: instead, it serves to honor both of his grandfathers, Anderson Shipp Truman and Solomon Young.

DWIGHT D. EISENHOWER Republican Party 1953–61
Vice president: Richard M. Nixon **First lady:** Mamie Geneva Doud
Born: October 14, 1890, Texas **Died:** March 28, 1969
Have You Heard? Dwight Eisenhower, a dedicated golfer, had a putting green installed on the White House lawn and eventually had all squirrels removed from the White House grounds because of the damage they were doing to the green.

JOHN F. KENNEDY Democratic Party 1961–63
Vice president: Lyndon B. Johnson **First lady:** Jacqueline Lee Bouvier
Born: May 29, 1917, Massachusetts **Died:** November 22, 1963
Have You Heard? John F. Kennedy, the only president to win a Pulitzer Prize (for his bestselling book *Profiles in Courage*), was the youngest president elected into office, and the youngest to die in office.

LYNDON B. JOHNSON Democratic Party 1963–69
Vice president: Hubert H. Humphrey **First lady:** Claudia Alta "Lady Bird" Taylor
Born: August 27, 1908, Texas **Died:** January 22, 1973
Have You Heard? Lyndon Johnson was such a big fan of the soft drink Fresca that he had a button installed on his desk in the Oval Office with the specific function of calling an aide to bring him the soda.

RICHARD M. NIXON Republican Party 1969–74
Vice presidents: Spiro T. Agnew, Gerald R. Ford **First lady:** Thelma "Pat" Ryan
Born: January 9, 1913, California **Died:** April 22, 1994
Have You Heard? In 1965, Richard Nixon turned down an offer for a job as a player's representative to the Major League Baseball Players Association, saying he was needed in politics.

GERALD R. FORD Republican Party 1974–77
Vice president: Nelson A. Rockefeller **First lady:** Elizabeth "Betty" Bloomer
Born: July 14, 1913, Nebraska **Died:** December 6, 2006
Have You Heard? Gerald Ford survived two assassination attempts; both were made in California during the month of September 1975, and both were made by women.

JIMMY (JAMES E.) CARTER Democratic Party 1977–81
Vice president: Walter F. Mondale **First lady:** Rosalynn Smith
Born: October 1, 1924, Georgia
Have You Heard? Jimmy Carter, one of three U.S. presidents who have been awarded the Nobel Peace Prize, was the first president who was born in a hospital.

RONALD REAGAN Republican Party 1981–89
Vice president: George H. W. Bush **First lady:** Nancy Davis
Born: February 6, 1911, Illinois **Died:** June 5, 2004
Have You Heard? From 1950 (the year they met) to well into the 1990s, Ronald Reagan wrote regular, romantic letters to his wife Nancy, sharing his love and thoughts of her throughout the many years of their marriage.

GEORGE H. W. BUSH Republican Party 1989–93
Vice president: J. Danforth Quayle **First lady:** Barbara Pierce
Born: June 12, 1924, Massachusetts
Have You Heard? When George Bush was a pilot for the navy during World War II, he was shot down while flying over the Pacific Ocean and saved by a submarine.

BILL (WILLIAM J.) CLINTON Democratic Party 1993–2001
Vice president: Albert Gore Jr. **First lady:** Hillary Rodham
Born: August 19, 1946, Arkansas
Have You Heard? Bill Clinton was a successful young saxophone player who briefly considered becoming a professional musician until the opportunity to meet John Kennedy during a high school trip with Boys Nation to the White House inspired him to aim for a life in public service.

GEORGE W. BUSH Republican Party 2001–08
Vice president: Richard B. Cheney **First lady:** Laura Welch
Born: July 6, 1946, Connecticut
Have You Heard? George W. Bush is the first president since Benjamin Harrison, in 1888, to be elected to the presidency without winning the popular vote.

BARACK H. OBAMA Democratic Party 2008–
Vice president: Joseph Biden Jr. **First lady:** Michelle Robinson
Born: August 4, 1961, Hawaii
Have You Heard? Barack Obama is the first African American president, and the first president born outside of the contiguous United States (in Hawaii).

FAMOUS FIRST LADIES

Martha Dandridge Custis Washington
The first of the First Ladies, Martha Washington was a private, unassuming woman whose primary concern was always the care and comfort of her family. Despite her desire to live a quiet life at home, she rose to the occasion of her position, following her General husband into the battlefield to spend a cold, dangerous winter with the troops in Valley Forge, and hosting many formal receptions and affairs of state once he became president. After her husband's death in 1799, she did guarantee a lasting privacy for them by burning their letters.

Abigail Smith Adams
Wife of one president and mother of another, Abigail Adams is best remembered through the many letters she and her husband shared during long separations as he served his country, proving that their relationship was fueled not only by enduring love but also by a deep intellectual connection, with John Adams seeking her council on many occasions, including those regarding political issues.

Dolley Todd Madison
Dolley Madison, a warm, welcoming, lively, and politically astute hostess who became the toast of Washington, more than compensated for her husband's relative lack of charm and remains to this day one of the most beloved First Ladies in history.

Mary Todd Lincoln
Mary Todd Lincoln was a southerner with a vivacious personality, a sharp wit, a powerful intelligence, and a strong opposition to slavery. Despite many early triumphs for her and her husband, her life was marked by tragedy as Lincoln was assassinated, three of her four children died young, and she slid into a world of mental and emotional anguish.

Anna Eleanor Roosevelt
Eleanor Roosevelt's lifelong activism in politics and advocacy for women and the underprivileged, and for human rights in general, made her not only a remarkable and memorable First Lady but also one of the most revered figures of the twentieth century.

Jacqueline Bouvier Kennedy Onassis

Jackie Kennedy was known and loved for her taste and intellect, her social graces, and her passion for culture and the arts that brought writers, artists, scientists, and musicians to the White House on a regular basis and created an unprecedented focus on culture in American society. Her courage in the face of her husband's assassination and the focus she placed on the lives of her children only contributed to the global admiration this elegant First Lady inspired.

Claudia "Lady Bird" Taylor Johnson

Lady Bird Johnson is known and revered for her lifelong advocacy for the conservation of natural resources and the environment and for the preservation and beautification of the nation's cities. She continued to follow this passion throughout her life, long after being First Lady, including the founding of the National Wildflower Research Center and work with many other organizations.

Elizabeth "Betty" Bloomer Ford

A strong and dignified woman who spent time as an accomplished modern dancer in her youth, Betty Ford has influenced the lives of millions with her support for women's rights, her frank openness about her successful battles with breast cancer and substance abuse, and the establishment of the Betty Ford Center for the treatment of drug and alcohol dependency.

Nancy Davis Reagan

Like her husband, Nancy Reagan began her career starring in Hollywood movies before turning her focus to her position as a political wife and activist. Nancy Reagan is known for her stylish dress and interest in fashion—particularly the color red—as well as her dedication to the fight against recreational drug use and founding of the "Just Say No" drug awareness campaign. As evidenced in the many letters they shared throughout their relationship, the Reagans enjoyed one of the most romantic presidential marriages.

Hillary Rodham Clinton

Hillary Clinton's career began well before she became First Lady with her work as a prominent lawyer and advocate that had her named two times as one of the 100 most influential lawyers in America. Her political career now continues to grow well after her run as First Lady ended, with eight years spent as a successful senator for New York, a close run as a leading candidate for the Democratic presidential nomination, and her current position as secretary of state in the cabinet of Barack Obama.

Laura Welch Bush

A former teacher and librarian, Laura Bush spent her two terms as First Lady sharing her passion and advocacy for the importance of reading and education for children. She was also a strong supporter for the rights of women, particularly for those of women in Afghanistan, following the attacks of September 11.

Michelle Robinson Obama

Michelle Obama, the first African American First Lady, is a Princeton- and Harvard-educated lawyer who left her work with a successful Chicago law firm to dedicate herself to a life of service. Her passions lie in raising her two daughters, supporting her husband in his political career, and working tirelessly for the causes that mean so much to her, including supporting military families and working mothers and encouraging all to embrace national service.

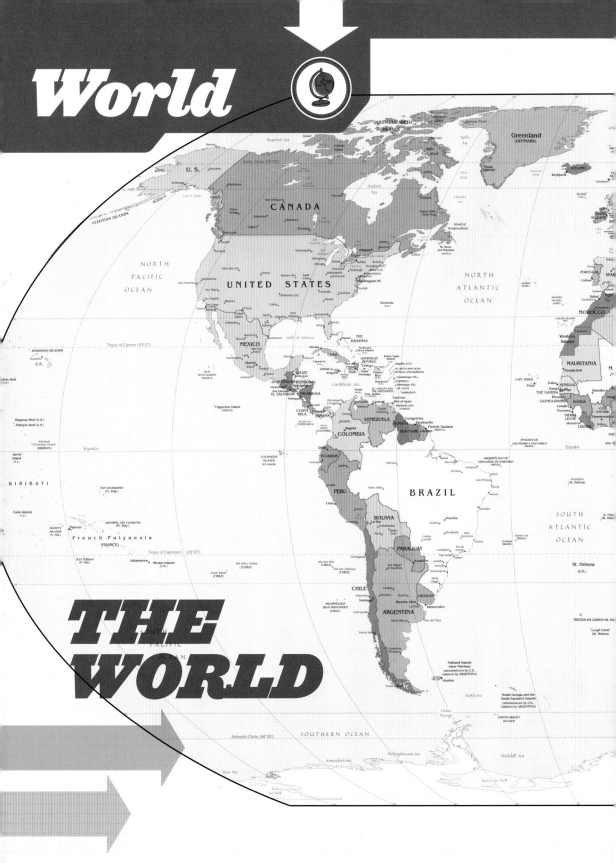

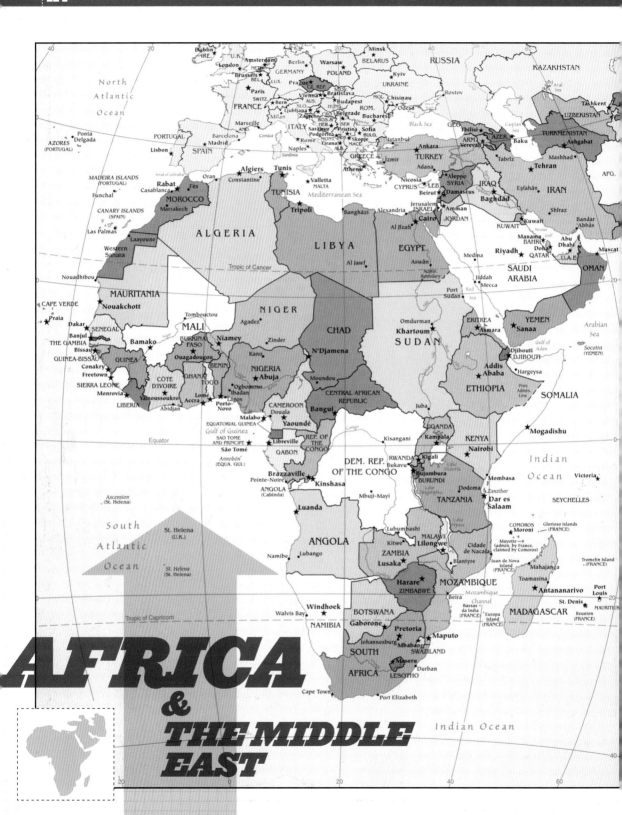

AFRICA & THE MIDDLE EAST

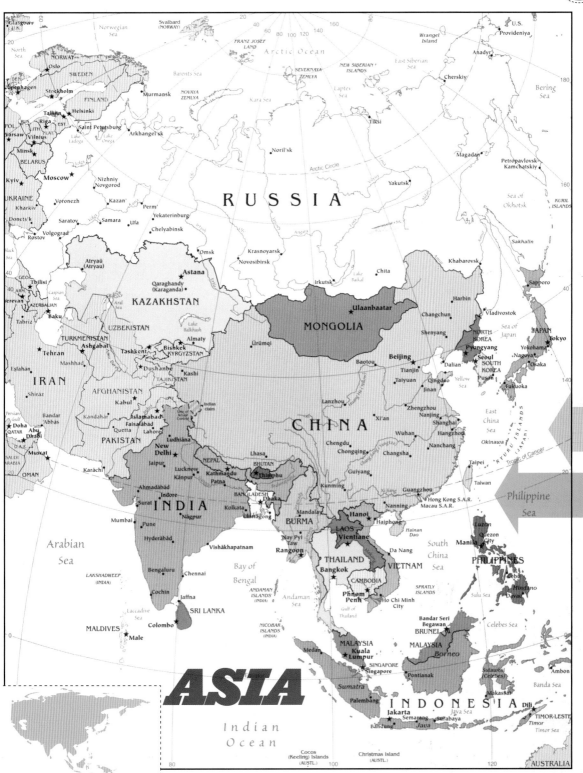

AUSTRALIA

INDONESIA

Banda Sea

INDONESIA

PAPUA NEW GUINEA

Solomon Sea

Dili
Denpasar   Kupang   East Timor
            Timor
Merauke   Daru
Port Moresby
Kupiano

Arafura Sea

Torres Strait

Timor Sea

Darwin

Gulf
of
Carpentaria

Weipa

Great Barrier Reef

Coral Sea

INDIAN
OCEAN

Katherine

Wyndham
Kununurra

Normanton
Forsayth

Cairns

Coral Sea
Islands
(AUSTRALIA)

Derby

NORTHERN

Townsville

Broome

Tennant
Creek

Charters
Towers

Ashmore and
Cartier Islands
(AUSTRALIA)

Port Hedland
Dampier
Karratha

Yarrie

TERRITORY

Mount Isa

Mackay

WESTERN

Tropic of Capricorn

QUEENSLAND

Newman

Alice Springs

Rockhampton

Paraburdoo

AUSTRALIA

Yulara

Yaraka

Bundaberg
Maryborough

Carnarvon

Gascoyne

Quilpie   Charleville

Meekatharra

Lake
Eyre

SOUTH

Brisbane
Gold Coast

Leonora

Coober Pedy

AUSTRALIA

Cunnamulla   Toowoomba

Lismore

Geraldton

Leigh
Creek

Bourke   Walgett

Armidale

Coffs Harbour

Kalgoorlie

Lake
Gairdner

Lake
Torrens

Broken
Hill

Cobar

Tamworth

Port Macquarie

Ceduna   Port Augusta
Whyalla

NEW SOUTH

Dubbo
Orange

Perth
Fremantle

Lake
Frome

Darling

WALES

Newcastle

Bunbury

Port Pirie

Mildura   Hillston

Esperance

Port Lincoln   Adelaide

Murray   Lachlan

Murrumbidgee

Sydney
Wollongong

Albany

Swan Hill

Wagga
Wagga

Canberra

Great Australian Bight

Bendigo
Ballarat

Albury

Australian
Capital
Territory

VICTORIA
Melbourne

Mount Gambier
Warrnambool   Geelong

Bairnsdale

Tasman Sea

Bass Strait

Devonport
Launceston

TASMANIA

INDIAN OCEAN

Hobart

Tasmania

Australia

——— International boundary
—·—·— State-level boundary
★ National capital
◉ State-level capital
+++ Railroad
=== Expressway
——— Road

0   500 Kilometers

0   500 Miles

Lambert Conformal Conic Projection, SP 13 S/42 S

EUROPE

NORTH AMERICA

Arctic Ocean

RUSSIA

East Siberian Sea

Chukchi Sea

Greenland Sea

Greenland (DENMARK)

Reykjavik

Nord

Alert

Ellesmere Island

QUEEN ELIZABETH ISLANDS

Qaanaaq (Thule)

Ilulissat (Jakobshavn)

Tasiilaq

Denmark Strait

Anadyr

Providenlya

Bering Strait

Nome

Barrow

Prudhoe Bay

Beaufort Sea

Banks Island

Resolute

Baffin Bay

Pond Inlet

Sisimiut (Holsteinsborg)

Bethel

UNITED STATES

Fairbanks

Inuvik

Victoria Island

Cambridge Bay

Gjoa Haven

Baffin Island

Davis Strait

Nuuk (Godthåb)

Qaqortoq (Julianehåb)

Bering Sea

Anchorage

Valdez

Dawson

Whitehorse

Arctic Circle

Great Bear Lake

Great Slave Lake

Iqaluit

Gulf of Alaska

Juneau

Fort Nelson

Lake Athabasca

Rankin Inlet

C A N A D A

Arviat

Hudson Bay

Kuujjuaq

Happy Valley-Goose Bay

Labrador Sea

Island of Newfoundland

Prince George

Fort McMurray

Churchill

Chisasibi

St. John's

North Pacific Ocean

Edmonton

Lake Winnipeg

Chicoutimi (Saguenay)

St. Pierre and Miquelon (FRANCE)

Sydney

Vancouver

Victoria

Seattle

Calgary

Saskatoon

Regina

Winnipeg

Thunder Bay

Moosonee

Sudbury

Ottawa

Québec

Montréal

Moncton

Fredericton

Charlottetown

Halifax

St. John

Portland

Fargo

Lake Superior

Lake Huron

Boston

Providence

Hartford

New York

Boise

Minneapolis

Lake Michigan

Milwaukee

Toronto

Hamilton

London

Detroit

Buffalo

Lake Erie

Lake Ontario

Philadelphia

Baltimore

Great Salt Lake

Salt Lake City

UNITED

Chicago

Cleveland

Columbus

Pittsburgh

Sacramento

Omaha

Indianapolis

Cincinnati

Washington, D.C.

Virginia Beach

San Francisco

San Jose

Fresno

Denver

Kansas City

Saint Louis

Louisville

Charlotte

Bermuda (U.K.)

STATES

Las Vegas

Los Angeles

San Diego

Phoenix

Albuquerque

Oklahoma City

Memphis

Nashville

Atlanta

Birmingham

North Atlantic Ocean

Tijuana

Mexicali

Tucson

El Paso

Dallas

Jacksonville

Ciudad Juárez

Austin

Houston

New Orleans

Orlando

Tampa

Hermosillo

Chihuahua

San Antonio

Miami

THE BAHAMAS

Nassau

Guadeloupe

Saltillo

Tropic of Cancer

Gulf of California

La Paz

Torreón

Culiacán

Monterrey

Matamoros

Gulf of Mexico

Havana

CUBA

HAITI

MEXICO

San Luis Potosí

Tampico

Cancun

Kingston

JAMAICA

Aguascalientes

Léon

Querétaro

Mérida

Guadalajara

Morelia

Toluca

Mexico

Veracruz

Bahía de Campeche

ISLAS REVILLAGIGEDO (MEXICO)

Puebla

Oaxaca

BELIZE

Belmopan

Caribbean Sea

Acapulco

Guatemala

GUATEMALA

San Salvador

EL SALVADOR

HONDURAS

Tegucigalpa

NICARAGUA

Managua

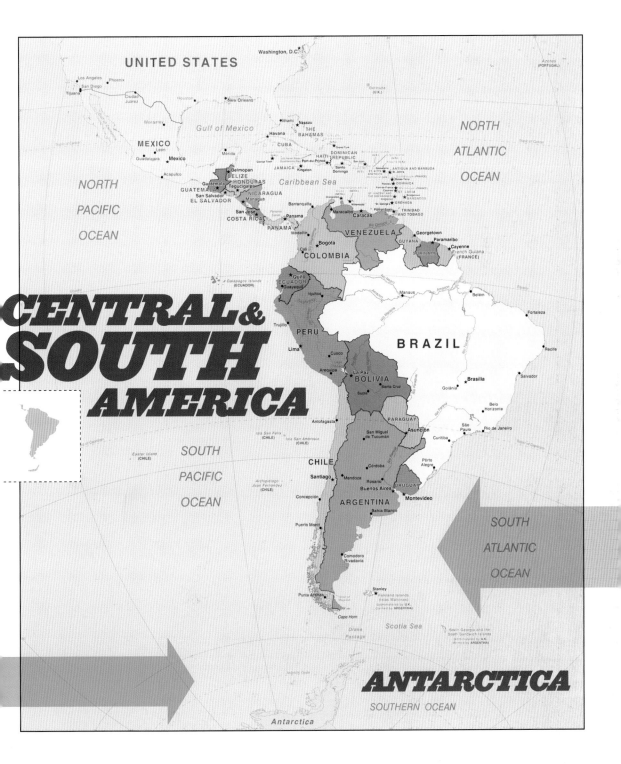

CENTRAL & SOUTH AMERICA

UNITED STATES

Washington, D.C.

Los Angeles
San Diego
Phoenix
Tijuana
Ciudad Juárez
Monterrey
Houston
New Orleans
Miami

Bermuda (U.K.)

Azores (PORTUGAL)

NORTH
ATLANTIC
OCEAN

Nassau
THE BAHAMAS
Havana
CUBA
Grand Turk
George Town
Kingston
Port-au-Prince
HAITI
DOMINICAN
REPUBLIC
Santo Domingo
San Juan

Gulf of Mexico

MEXICO
León
Guadalajara
Mexico
Acapulco
Mérida

NORTH
PACIFIC
OCEAN

Caribbean Sea

Belmopan
BELIZE
GUATEMALA
Guatemala
HONDURAS
Tegucigalpa
San Salvador
EL SALVADOR
NICARAGUA
Managua
San José
COSTA RICA
Panama
Panama Canal
PANAMA

JAMAICA

ANTIGUA AND BARBUDA
St. John's
DOMINICA
ST. KITTS AND NEVIS
ST. LUCIA
BARBADOS
ST. VINCENT AND
THE GRENADINES
GRENADA
TRINIDAD AND TOBAGO
Port-of-Spain

Barranquilla
Maracaibo
Caracas

VENEZUELA
Georgetown
GUYANA
Paramaribo
SURINAME
Cayenne
French Guiana (FRANCE)

Medellín

COLOMBIA
Cali
Bogotá

Galápagos Islands (ECUADOR)
Quito
ECUADOR
Guayaquil
Iquitos

Manaus
Belém

Equator

Fortaleza

Trujillo

PERU
Lima
Cusco
Arequipa

BRAZIL

Recife

La Paz
BOLIVIA
Sucre
Santa Cruz

Goiânia
Brasília

Salvador

Antofagasta

Belo Horizonte

PARAGUAY

SOUTH
PACIFIC
OCEAN

Isla San Félix (CHILE)
Isla San Ambrosio (CHILE)
Easter Island (CHILE)
Archipiélago Juan Fernández (CHILE)

San Miguel de Tucumán
Asunción
São Paulo
Rio de Janeiro
Curitiba

CHILE
Córdoba
Santiago
Mendoza
Rosario
Buenos Aires
Concepción
Pórto Alegre
URUGUAY
Montevideo

ARGENTINA
Bahía Blanca

Puerto Montt

SOUTH
ATLANTIC
OCEAN

Comodoro Rivadavia

Punta Arenas
Stanley
Falkland Islands (Islas Malvinas)
(administered by U.K.,
claimed by ARGENTINA)

Cape Horn

South Georgia and the
South Sandwich Islands
(administered by U.K.,
claimed by ARGENTINA)

Drake Passage
Scotia Sea

ANTARCTICA

SOUTHERN OCEAN

Antarctica

WOMEN IN HISTORY

Cleopatra

Cleopatra, one of Egypt's pharaohs, lived from 69 BC to 30 BC. She had a son with Julius Caesar, which helped her remain the ruler. After Caesar was assassinated, she joined with Mark Antony to fight against Caesar's chosen heir's claim to become the ruler. She had three children with Mark Antony and later married her brothers but did not have children with them. She committed suicide by allowing a poisonous snake to bite her.

Joan of Arc

Joan was born a peasant in France in 1412. As a young girl Joan claimed she had visions from God telling her to help reclaim France from England. She led France's army to some important victories but, in 1431, was burned at the stake for being a heretic (someone who goes against established church beliefs). Twenty-four years after her death, she was declared innocent and made a martyr (someone who sacrifices his or her life for others) in the Catholic Church. She is now known as Saint Joan.

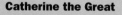

Helen Keller

Helen Keller was born in 1880 and at nineteen months developed an illness that left her both blind and deaf. By the time Helen was seven, she'd developed more than 60 signs that she would use to communicate. Helen's parents were put in touch with Alexander Graham Bell, who recommended the Perkins Institute for the Blind in Boston. This led Helen to Anne Sullivan, who would be her friend and teacher for forty-nine years. Helen was the first deaf and blind person to graduate with a Bachelor of Arts from a college (Radcliffe).

Catherine the Great

Catherine was born in 1729 and was the empress of Russia from 1762 to 1796. Under her rule, the Russian Empire expanded; she improved the administration and worked to modernize Russia, leading it to be considered one of Europe's great powers. Catherine caused a lot of gossip and even scandal due to the relationships she kept. She was friends with those who worked to improve life for the poorest of Russia's people, the serfs, but she eventually found it impractical to do so.

Anne Frank

Annelies "Anne" Frank was a Jewish German girl, born in 1929, who kept a diary during the years she was in hiding in Amsterdam because of the Holocaust (a mass extermination of Jews, led by the Nazis during World War II). She and her family (and another family and friend) were betrayed after two years and sent to concentration camps. She died from typhus seven months after her capture, in 1945. Her book, *The Diary of a Young Girl*, remains a classic, and her story has been turned into a play as well as a movie.

Susan B. Anthony

Susan B. Anthony lived from 1820 to 1906. She learned to read at age three. Her father did not allow her to play with toys; he thought they would distract her soul. Anthony was a leading advocate for women's rights and fought for women's right to vote. She gave lectures all over the United States and Europe.

Pocahontas

Pocahontas, a Native American, lived from 1595 to 1617. Her father, Wa-hun-sen-a-cawh, was the chief of the Powhatan tribe. Legend has it that when John Smith was brought before Wa-hun-sen-a-cawh and about to be executed, his life was saved when Pocahontas threw her body in the way. Later, Pocahontas married an Englishman named John Rolfe, was baptized, and became known as Rebecca Rolfe.

Amelia Earhart

Amelia Earhart was born in 1897 and believed to have died sometime after July 2, 1937, when the plane she was flying over the Pacific Ocean disappeared. The plane has never been recovered. Earhart was officially declared dead in 1939. She was the first woman to fly solo across the Atlantic Ocean, set many other flying records, and wrote bestselling books about her flights.

Marie Curie

Marie Curie lived from 1867 to 1934. She was both a chemist and physicist, who grew up in Poland and later lived in France. She created the theory of radioactivity and discovered two new elements: polonium and radium. Curie became the first person ever to win two Nobel Prizes and was also the first female professor at the University of Paris.

Amelia

FAMOUS ACTIVISTS

EQUALITY

ending apartheid

Martin Luther

Martin Luther lived from 1483 to 1546. He started the Protestant Reformation, which was when many new (Protestant) religions sprung up as they broke away from Catholicism. The pope asked him to retract all his writings, but he refused and was excommunicated. His followers are called Lutherans.

Great soul

Mohandas K. Gandhi

Mohandas K. Gandhi is often referred to as Mahatma Gandhi, *mahatma* meaning, "great soul." Gandhi was both a political and spiritual leader in India. He lived from 1869 to 1948. He taught others how to effect change through civil disobedience—refusal to obey certain rules while remaining nonviolent. He helped to reduce poverty and improve the rights of women and those considered "untouchable."

Mother Teresa

Agnes Gonxha Bojaxhiu was a girl from Albania who became a Catholic nun in 1931 and chose the name Teresa for herself, after Therese de Lisieux, the patron saint of missionaries. Mother Teresa lived from 1910 to 1997. She started the Missionaries of Charity in Calcutta, India, and worked for nearly fifty years with India's poorest and sickest people.

Nelson Mandela

Nelson Mandela was born in 1918 in South Africa. He was the president of South Africa and the first to be elected in a democratic election. Before being president, Mandela worked to end apartheid (a system of racial segregation). The courts convicted him on charges of sabotage, and he spent 27 years in prison. He has received more than 100 awards, including the Nobel Peace Prize.

Mother Teresa

KIDS WHO MADE A DIFFERENCE

Young Mozart

Wolfgang Amadeus Mozart lived from 1756 to 1791. His father was a prominent violin teacher, and taught him how to play the harpsichord, piano, and violin at a very young age. It is said he could teach himself complicated pieces in half an hour. By five, Mozart was composing his own music. As a child he performed before European royalty, while living in Salzburg, Austria.

Louis Braille

Louis Braille lived from 1809 to 1852 in France. At the age of three, he accidentally blinded one eye by stabbing himself with one of his father's workshop tools. He later lost his sight in his other eye due to sympathetic opthalmia (inflammation in both eyes due to trauma in one). At ten, he went to the National Institute for the Blind in Paris and was taught how to read using a system of raised letters, but kids were not taught to write. In 1821, he invented his own raised dot system using his father's awl, the same tool that had blinded him. That system of raised dots is known as Braille.

Young Picasso

Pablo Picasso lived from 1881 to 1973. He grew up in Spain but spent much of his life in France. Picasso was considered to be the greatest artist of the twentieth century. By the age of ten he'd done his first painting, and at fifteen he was admitted to Barcelona's School of Fine Arts. He produced more than 20,000 works of art, in many different media.

PABLO PICASSO
20,000 works of Art

GEOGRAPHY

HOW WE FOUND EVERYTHING: A TIME LINE OF WORLD EXPLORATION

Approximately 1000 AD: Leif Eriksson, hailing from Iceland, leads the Vikings to first discover an area in North America that he names Vinland. The exact location of Vinland is unknown, but it is thought to be in the northeastern sections of Canada and the United States.

1271–95: Marco Polo, a Venetian merchant, travels throughout Asia and introduces Europeans to Central Asia and China.

1488: Bartholomeu Dias, a Portuguese nobleman, is the first European to sail around the Cape of Good Hope, at the southernmost tip of Africa.

1492: Christopher Columbus, an Italian navigator and explorer, sets sail from Spain on the first of several voyages across the Atlantic Ocean and lands in the Americas.

1497: John Cabot, a Venetian navigator and explorer, who in Italy is known as Giovanni Caboto, becomes the second European to sail to North America (which at the time was thought to be Asia) on a voyage funded by King Henry VII and claims the land he discovered for England.

1497–1504: Amerigo Vespucci, an Italian businessman and explorer, leads several voyages to Central and South America. He is one of the first explorers to realize that they are not parts of Asia, but rather of a "New World." The Americas get their name from his first name.

1497–99: Vasco da Gama, a Portuguese count and explorer, commands the first ships to sail from Europe to India, via Africa and the Cape of Good Hope.

1513: Juan Ponce de León, a Spanish explorer and politician, heads the first European voyage to Florida, which he then names.

1513: Vasco Núñez de Balboa, a Spanish explorer and conquistador, crosses Panama to the Pacific Ocean as the first explorer to approach the Pacific from the New World (the Americas).

1519–21: Ferdinand Magellan, a Portuguese maritime explorer, leads the first expedition across the Pacific Ocean. Magellan is killed in the Philippines, but his expedition continues to become the first to circumnavigate the globe.

1519–36: Hernán Cortés, a Spanish conquistador, conquers the Aztec Empire and part of Mexico, helping to begin the Spanish colonization of the Americas.

1524: Giovanni da Verrazano, an Italian explorer funded by the French, becomes the first European since the Vikings to explore the east coast of North America, including what would become known as the New York Harbor and the Hudson River.

1532–33: Francisco Pizarro, a Spanish conquistador, explores the west coast of South America and conquers the Incan Empire, which would become Peru.

1534: Jacques Cartier, a French explorer, explores what is now Canada's St. Lawrence River and claims many parts of North America for France.

1539–42: Hernando de Soto, a Spanish explorer and conquistador, leads the first European expedition into the southeastern parts of what would become the United States and discovers the Mississippi River.

1577–80: Sir Francis Drake, an English ship captain and politician, unintentionally circumnavigates the world by sailing ship.

1603–13: Samuel de Champlain, French navigator and diplomat, explores North America and, like Jacques Cartier before him, claims many of the northern parts for France, establishing what would eventually become Quebec City. French is still spoken in much of Canada today.

1609–11: Henry Hudson, an English sailor and navigator, explores some of the northeastern waters of what would become the United States, including the Hudson River and Hudson Bay, which are named after him.

1682: René-Robert Cavelier, Sieur (Lord) de La Salle, a French explorer, travels through the Great Lakes region, the Mississippi River, and the Gulf of Mexico, claiming all of the Mississippi River basin—which he calls the Louisiana Territory—for France.

1768–79: James Cook, a British cartographer and navy captain, leads a successful sea expedition around the world and is the first European to explore new parts of the Pacific Ocean and the Far East, including Hawaii and the Antarctic Circle.

1769–75: Daniel Boone, an American pioneer, explores the wilds of Kentucky, blazing trails in the territory and encountering Native Americans several times along the way.

1804–06: Meriwether Lewis and William Clark, American soldiers and explorers, lead the first American transcontinental expedition, 8,000 miles across the wilderness of America, from St. Louis to the Pacific coast and back. They are accompanied by Sacagawea, a Native American woman from the Shoshone tribe whose knowledge of the land and ability to communicate with the native tribes serves them well.

Clark

1849–59: David Livingstone, a doctor, missionary, and explorer, dedicates years of his life to explorations of southern and central Africa, using the people-skills learned in his missionary work to establish the trust of various tribal chiefs in his travels.

1908–09: Robert Peary and Matthew Henson, a team of American explorers who traveled in Greenland and the Arctic region, become the first to almost reach the North Pole (today it is widely suspected that they missed the mark by 30 to 60 miles).

1910–12: Roald Amundsen, a Norwegian explorer, heads the first Antarctic expedition to make it to the South Pole.

1925–55: Richard E. Byrd, an American explorer of the polar regions, devotes decades of his life to explorations of Greenland, the Arctic, and Antarctica, by air and by water.

1936–80: Jacques-Yves Cousteau, a French explorer, filmmaker, and environmentalist, makes tremendous strides in the study and protection of ocean life and helps develop the Aqua-Lung, which enables divers to spend hours deep beneath the sea.

1927: Charles A. Lindbergh, an American aviator and explorer, becomes world famous for his nonstop solo flight across the Atlantic from Long Island to Paris and uses this status to make many contributions to the improvement and promotion of U.S. commercial aviation.

1962: John Glenn, an American astronaut and politician, becomes the first American to orbit the earth in space and goes on to an esteemed career in the military and politics. In 1998, at seventy-seven years old, he sets another record, becoming the oldest person to fly in space.

1963: Valentina Tereshkova, a Soviet cosmonaut, becomes the first woman to fly in space.

1969: Neil Armstrong, an American aviator and astronaut, becomes the first person to set foot on the moon and makes the famous assertion: "That's one small step for man, one giant leap for mankind."

1983: Sally Ride, an American physicist and NASA astronaut, becomes the first American woman to enter space.

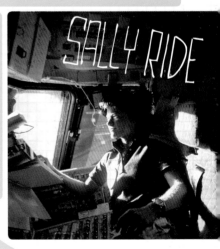

THE NATIONS

[POPULATION FIGURES ARE JULY 2009 ESTIMATES FROM THE CIA WORLD FACTBOOK]

Afghanistan

World Region: Asia

Capital: Kabul

Population: 33,609,937

Area: 250,000 square miles (647,500 sq km)

Languages: Afghan Persian (or Dari), Pashto

Currency: afghani

Albania

World Region: Europe

Capital: Tirana

Population: 3,639,453

Area: 11,100 square miles (28,748 sq km)

Languages: Albanian, Greek

Currency: lek

Algeria

World Region: Africa

Capital: Algiers

Population: 34,178,188

Area: 919,590 square miles (2,381,740 sq km)

Languages: Arabic, French, Berber dialects

Currency: Algerian dinar

Andorra

World Region: Europe

Capital: Andorra la Vella

Population: 83,888

Area: 181 square miles (468 sq km)

Languages: Catalan, French, Castilian

Currency: euro

Angola

World Region: Africa

Capital: Luanda

Population: 12,799,293

Area: 481,3551 square miles (1,246,700 sq km)

Languages: Portuguese, Bantu

Currency: kwanza

Antigua and Barbuda

World Region: Caribbean

Capital: Saint John's

Population: 85,632

Area: 171 square miles (443 sq km)

Language: English

Currency: East Caribbean dollar

Argentina

World Region: South America

Capital: Buenos Aires

Population: 40,913,584

Area: 1,068,296 square miles (2,766,890 sq km)

Languages: Spanish, Italian, English, German, French

Currency: Argentine peso

Armenia
World Region: Asia

Capital: Yerevan

Population: 2,967,004

Area: 11,506 square miles (29,800 sq km)

Language: Armenian

Currency: dram

Australia
World Region: Oceania (Pacific Ocean)

Capital: Canberra

Population: 21,262,641

Area: 2,967,893 square miles (7,686,850 sq km)

Language: English

Currency: Australian dollar

Austria
World Region: Europe

Capital: Vienna

Population: 8,210,281

Area: 32,382 square miles (83,870 sq km)

Language: German

Currency: euro

Azerbaijan
World Region: Asia

Capital: Baku

Population: 8,238,672

Area: 33,436 square miles (86,600 sq km)

Languages: Azerbaijani, Lezgi, Russian, Armenian

Currency: Azerbaijani manat

Bahamas
World Region: Caribbean

Capital: Nassau

Population: 309,156

Area: 5,382 square miles (13,940 sq km)

Languages: English, Creole

Currency: Bahamian dollar

Bahrain
World Region: Middle East

Capital: Manama

Population: 727,785

Area: 257 square miles (665 sq km)

Languages: Arabic, English, Farsi, Urdu

Currency: Bahraini dinar

Bangladesh
World Region: Asia

Capital: Dhaka

Population: 156,050,883

Area: 55,598 square miles (144,000 sq km)

Languages: Bangla, English

Currency: taka

Barbados
World Region: Caribbean

Capital: Bridgetown

Population: 284,589

Area: 166 square miles (431 sq km)

Language: English

Currency: Barbadian dollar

Belarus
World Region: Europe

Capital: Minsk

Population: 9,648,533

Area: 80,154 square miles (207,600 sq km)

Languages: Belarusian, Russian

Currency: Belarusian ruble

Belgium
World Region: Europe

Capital: Brussels

Population: 10,414,336

Area: 11,787 square miles (30,528 sq km)

Languages: Dutch, French, German

Currency: euro

Belize
World Region: Central America

Capital: Belmopan

Population: 307, 899

Area: 8,867 square miles (22,966 sq km)

Languages: English, Spanish, Creole, Mayan, Garifuna

Currency: Belizean dollar

Benin
World Region: Africa

Capital: Porto-Novo

Population: 8,791,832

Area: 43,483 square miles (112,620 sq km)

Languages: French, Fon, Yoruba

Currency: CFA franc

Bhutan
World Region: Asia

Capital: Thimphu

Population: 691,141

Area: 18,147 square miles (47,000 sq km)

Language: Dzongkha

Currency: ngultrum

Bolivia
World Region: South America

Capital: La Paz (seat of government); Sucre (legal capital and seat of judiciary)

Population: 9,775,246

Area: 424,162 square miles (1,098,580 sq km)

Languages: Spanish, Quechua, Aymara

Currency: boliviano

Bosnia and Herzegovina
World Region: Europe

Capital: Sarajevo

Population: 4,613,414

Area: 19,741 square miles (51,129 sq km)

Languages: Bosnian, Croatian, Serbian

Currency: marka

Botswana
World Region: Africa

Capital: Gaborone

Population: 1,990,876

Area: 231,803 square miles (600,370 sq km)

Languages: Setswana, Kalanga, Sekgalagadi, English

Currency: pula

Brazil
World Region: South America

Capital: Brasilia

Population: 198,739,269

Area: 3,286,470 square miles (8,511,965 sq km)

Languages: Portuguese, Spanish, English

Currency: real

Brunei
World Region: Southeast Asia

Capital: Bandar Seri Begawan

Population: 388,190

Area: 2,228 square miles (5,770 sq km)

Languages: Malay, English, Chinese

Currency: Bruneian dollar

Bulgaria
World Region: Europe

Capital: Sofia

Population: 7,204,687

Area: 42,822 square miles (110,910 sq km)

Languages: Bulgarian, Turkish, Roma

Currency: lev

Burkina Faso
World Region: Africa

Capital: Ouagadougou

Population: 15,746,232

Area: 105,860 square miles (274,200 sq km)

Languages: French, African languages

Currency: CFA franc

Burundi
World Region: Africa

Capital: Bujumbura

Population: 8,988,091

Area: 10,745 square miles (27,830 sq km)

Languages: Kirundi, French, Swahili

Currency: Burundi franc

Cambodia
World Region: Southeast Asia

Capital: Phnom Penh

Population: 14,494,293

Area: 69,900 square miles (181,040 sq km)

Languages: Khmer, French, English

Currency: riel

Cameroon
World Region: Africa

Capital: Yaounde

Population: 18,879,301

Area: 183,567 square miles (475,440 sq km)

Languages: English, French, African languages

Currency: CFA franc

Canada
World Region: North America

Capital: Ottawa

Population: 33,487,208

Area: 3,855,081 square miles (9,984,670 sq km)

Languages: English, French

Currency: Canadian dollar

Cape Verde
World Region: Africa

Capital: Praia

Population: 429,474

Area: 1,557 square miles (4,033 sq km)

Languages: Portuguese, Crioulo

Currency: Cape Verdean escudo

Central African Republic
World Region: Africa

Capital: Bangui

Population: 4,511,488

Area: 240,534 square miles (622,984 sq km)

Languages: French, Sangho, African languages

Currency: CFA franc

Chad
World Region: Africa

Capital: N'Djamena

Population: 10,329,208

Area: 495,752 square miles (1,284,000 sq km)

Languages: French, Arabic, Sara

Currency: CFA franc

Chile
World Region: South America

Capital: Santiago

Population: 16,601,707

Area: 292,258 square miles (756,950 sq km)

Languages: Spanish, Mapundungun, German, English

Currency: Chilean peso

China
World Region: Asia

Capital: Beijing

Population: 1,338,612,968

Area: 3,705,386 square miles (9,596,960 sq km)

Language: Chinese (Mandarin and other dialects)

Currency: renminbi (yuan)

Colombia
World Region: South America

Capital: Bogota

Population: 45,644,023

Area: 439,733 square miles (1,138,910 sq km)

Language: Spanish

Currency: Colombian peso

Comoros
World Region: Africa

Capital: Moroni

Population: 752,438

Area: 838 square miles (2,170 sq km)

Languages: Arabic, French, Shikomoro

Currency: Comoran franc

Congo, Democratic Republic of the
World Region: Africa

Capital: Kinshasa

Population: 68,692,542

Area: 905,563 square miles (2,345,410 sq km)

Languages: French, Lingala, Kingwana, Kikongo, Tshiluba

Currency: Congolese franc

Congo, Republic of the
World Region: Africa

Capital: Brazzaville

Population: 4,012,809

Area: 132,046 square miles (342,000 sq km)

Languages: French, Lingala, Monokutuba, Kikongo and other dialects

Currency: CFA franc

Costa Rica
World Region: Central America

Capital: San Jose

Population: 4,253,877

Area: 19,730 square miles (51,100 sq km)

Languages: Spanish, English

Currency: Costa Rican colon

Côte d'Ivoire
World Region: Africa

Capital: Yamoussoukro

Population: 20,617,068

Area: 124,502 sq. mi (322,460 sq. km)

Language: French, African dialects

Currency: CFA franc

Croatia
World Region: Europe

Capital: Zagreb

Population: 4,489,409

Area: 21,831 sq. mi (56,542 sq. km)

Language: Croatian

Currency: kuna

Cuba
World Region: The Caribbean

Capital: Havana

Population: 11,451,652

Area: 42,803 sq. mi
(110,860 sq. km)

Language: Spanish

Currency: Cuban peso

Cyprus
World Region: Middle East

Capital: Nicosia

Population: 796,740

Area: 3,571 sq. mi
(9,250 sq. km)

Language: Greek, Turkish

Currency: euro

Czech Republic
World Region: Europe

Capital: Prague

Population: 10,211,904

Area: 30,450 sq. mi
(78,866 sq. km)

Language: Czech, Slovak

Currency: Czech koruna

Denmark
World Region: Europe

Capital: Copenhagen

Population: 5,500,510

Area: 16,639 sq. mi
(43,094 sq. km)

Language: Danish, English,
Faroese, Greenlandic

Currency: Danish krone

Djibouti
World Region: Africa

Capital: Djibouti

Population: 516,055

Area: 8,880 sq. mi
(23,000 sq. km)

Language: French, Arabic, Somali,
Afar

Currency: Djiboutian franc

Dominica
World Region: The Caribbean

Capital: Roseau

Population: 72,660

Area: 291 sq. mi
(754 sq. km)

Language: English, French patois

Currency: East Caribbean dollar

Dominican Republic
World Region: The Caribbean

Capital: Santo Domingo

Population: 9,650,054

Area: 18,815 sq. mi
(48,730 sq. km)

Language: Spanish

Currency: Dominican peso

East Timor
World Region: Southeast Asia

Capital: Dili

Population: 1,131,612

Area: 5,794 sq. mi
(15,007 sq. km)

Language: Tetum, Portuguese,
Indonesian, English

Currency: U.S. dollar

Ecuador
World Region: South America

Capital: Quito

Population: 14,573,101

Area: 109,483 sq. mi
(283,560 sq. km)

Language: Spanish, Amerindian
languages

Currency: U.S. dollar

Egypt

World Region: Africa

Capital: Cairo

Population: 83,082,869

Area: 386,660 sq. mi
(1,001,450 sq. km)

Language: Arabic, English, French

Currency: Egyptian pound

El Salvador

World Region: Central America

Capital: San Salvador

Population: 7,185,218

Area: 8,124 sq. mi
(21,040 sq. km)

Language: Spanish, Nahua

Currency: U.S. dollar

Equatorial Guinea

World Region: Africa

Capital: Malabo

Population: 633,441

Area: 10,830 sq. mi
(28,051 sq. km)

Language: Spanish, French,
Fang, Bubi

Currency: CFA franc

Eritrea

World Region: Africa

Capital: Asmara

Population: 5,647,168

Area: 46,842 sq. mi
(121,320 sq. km)

Language: Afar, Arabic, Tigre,
Kunama. Tigrinya

Currency: nafka

Estonia

World Region: Europe

Capital: Tallinn

Population: 1,299,371

Area: 17,462 sq. mi
(45,226 sq. km)

Language: Estonian, Russian

Currency: Estonian kroon

Ethiopia

World Region: Africa

Capital: Addis Ababa

Population: 85,237,338

Area: 435,184 sq. mi
(1,127,127 sq. km)

Language: Amarigna, Oromigna,
Tigrigna, Somaligna, English,
others

Currency: birr

Fiji

World Region: Oceania

Capital: Suva

Population: 944,720

Area: 7,054 sq. mi
(18,270 sq. km)

Language: English, Fijian,
Hindustani

Currency: Fijian dollar

Finland

World Region: Europe

Capital: Helsinki

Population: 5,250,275

Area: 130,558 sq. mi
(338,145 sq. km)

Language: Finnish, Swedish

Currency: euro

France

World Region: Europe

Capital: Paris

Population: 64,057,792

Area: 211,208 sq. mi
(547,030 sq. km)

Language: French

Currency: euro

Gabon
World Region: Africa

Capital: Libreville

Population: 1,514,993

Area: 103,346 sq. mi
(267,667 sq. km)

Language: French, Fang, Myene,
Nzebi, Bapounou/Eschira,
Bandjabi

Currency: CFA franc

The Gambia
World Region: Africa

Capital: Banjul

Population: 1,782,893

Area: 4,363 sq. mi
(11,300 sq. km)

Language: English, Madinka,
Wolof, Fula

Currency: Dalasi

Georgia
World Region: Asia

Capital: T'bilisi

Population: 4,615,807

Area: 26,911 sq. mi
(69,700 sq. km)

Language: Georgian, Russian,
Armenian, Azeri, Abkhaz

Currency: lari

Germany
World Region: Europe

Capital: Berlin

Population: 82,329,758

Area: 137,846 sq. mi
(357,021 sq. km)

Language: German

Currency: euro

Ghana
World Region: Africa

Capital: Accra

Population: 23,832,495

Area: 92,456 sq. mi
(239,460 sq. km)

Language: English, Asante, Ewe,
Fante, Boron, Dagomba, Dangme

Currency: cedi

Greece
World Region: Europe

Capital: Athens

Population: 10,737,428

Area: 50,942 sq. mi
(131,940 sq. km)

Language: Greek, English, French

Currency: euro

Grenada
World Region: The Caribbean

Capital: Saint George's

Population: 90,739

Area: 133 sq. mi
(344 sq. km)

Language: English, French patois

Currency: East Caribbean dollar

Guatemala
World Region: Central America

Capital: Guatemala

Population: 13,276,517

Area: 42,042 sq. mi
(108,890 sq. km)

Language: Spanish, Amerindian
languages

Currency: quetzal, U.S. dollar

Guinea
World Region: Africa

Capital: Conakry

Population: 10,057,975

Area: 94,925 sq. mi
(245,857 sq. km)

Language: French, native
languages

Currency: Guinean franc

Guinea–Bissau
World Region: Africa

Capital: Bissau

Population: 1,533,964

Area: 13,946 sq. mi
(36,120 sq. km)

Language: Portuguese, Crioulo,
African languages

Currency: CFA franc

Guyana
World Region: South America

Capital: Georgetown

Population: 772,298

Area: 83,000 sq. mi
(214,970 sq. km)

Language: English, Amerindian
dialects, Creole, Caribbean
Hindustani, Urdu

Currency: Guyanese dollar

Haiti
World Region: The Caribbean

Capital: Port-au-Prince

Population: 9,035,536

Area: 10,714 sq. mi
(27,750 sq. km)

Language: French, Creole

Currency: gourde

Honduras
World Region: Central America

Capital: Tegucigalpa

Population: 7,792,854

Area: 43,278 sq. mi
(112,090 sq. km)

Language: Spanish, Amerindian

Currency: lempira

Hungary
World Region: Europe

Capital: Budapest

Population: 9,905,596

Area: 35,919 sq. mi
(93,030 sq. km)

Language: Hungarian

Currency: forint

Iceland
World Region: Europe

Capital: Reykjavik

Population: 306,694

Area: 39,768 sq. mi
(103,000 sq. km)

Language: Icelandic, English,
German, Nordic languages

Currency: Icelandic krona

India
World Region: Asia

Capital: New Delhi

Population: 1,166,079,217

Area: 1,269,338 sq. mi
(3,287,590 sq. km)

Language: Hindi, English, Bengali,
Telugu, Marathi, Tamil, Urdu

Currency: Indian rupee

Indonesia
World Region: Southeast Asia

Capital: Jakarta

Population: 240,271,522

Area: 741,096 sq. mi
(1,919,440 sq. km)

Language: Bahasa Indonesia,
English, Dutch, Javanese

Currency: Indonesian rupiah

Iran
World Region: Middle East

Capital: Tehran

Population: 66,429,284

Area: 636,679 sq. mi
(1,649,000 sq. km)

Language: Persian, Turkic, Kurdish

Currency: Iranian rial

Iraq
World Region: Middle East

Capital: Baghdad

Population: 28,945,657

Area: 168,753 sq. mi
(437,072 sq. km)

Language: Arabic, Kurdish,
Turkoman, Assyrian, Armenian

Currency: new Iraqi dinar

Ireland
World Region: Europe

Capital: Dublin

Population: 4,203,200

Area: 27,135 sq. mi
(70,280 sq. km)

Language: English, Irish (Gaelic
or Gaeilge)

Currency: euro

Israel
World Region: Middle East

Capital: Jerusalem

Population: 7,233,701

Area: 8,019 sq. mi
(20,770 sq. km)

Language: Hebrew, Arabic, English

Currency: new Israeli shekel

Italy
World Region: Europe

Capital: Rome

Population: 58,126,212

Area: 116,305 sq. mi
(301,230 sq. km)

Language: Italian, German,
French, Slovene

Currency: euro

Jamaica
World Region: The Caribbean

Capital: Kingston

Population: 2,825,928

Area: 4,244 sq. mi
(10,991 sq. km)

Language: English, English patois

Currency: Jamaican dollar

Japan
World Region: Asia

Capital: Tokyo

Population: 127,078,679

Area: 145,882 sq. mi
(377,835 sq. km)

Language: Japanese

Currency: yen

Jordan
World Region: Middle East

Capital: Amman

Population: 6,342,948

Area: 35,637 sq. mi
(92,300 sq. km)

Language: Arabic, English

Currency: Jordanian dinar

Kazakhstan
World Region: Asia

Capital: Astana

Population: 15,399,437

Area: 1,049 sq. mi
(2,717,300 sq. km)

Language: Kazakh, Russian

Currency: tenge

Kenya
World Region: Africa

Capital: Nairobi

Population: 39,002,772

Area: 224,961 sq. mi
(582,650 sq. km)

Language: English, Kiswahili,
indigenous languages

Currency: Kenyan shilling

Kiribati
World Region: Oceania

Capital: Tarawa

Population: 112,850

Area: 313 sq. mi
(811 sq. km)

Language: I-Kiribati, English

Currency: Australian dollar

Korea, North
World Region: Asia

Capital: Pyongyang

Population: 22,665,345

Area: 46,540 sq. mi
(120,540 sq. km)

Language: Korean

Currency: North Korean won

Korea, South
World Region: Asia

Capital: Seoul

Population: 48,508,972

Area: 38,023 sq. mi
(98,480 sq. km)

Language: Korean, English

Currency: South Korean won

Kosovo
World Region: Europe

Capital: Pristina

Population: 1,804,838

Area: 4,203 sq. mi
(10,887 sq. km)

Language: Albanian, Serbian,
Bosnian, Turkish, Roma

Currency: euro, Serbian dinar

Kuwait
World Region: Middle East

Capital: Kuwait

Population: 2,691,158

Area: 6,880 sq. mi
(17,820 sq. km)

Language: Arabic, English

Currency: Kuwaiti dinar

Kyrgyzstan
World Region: Asia

Capital: Bishkek

Population: 5,431,747

Area: 76,641 sq. mi
(198,500 sq. km)

Language: Kyrgyz, Uzbek, Russian

Currency: Kyrgyzstani som

Laos
World Region: Southeast Asia

Capital: Vientiane

Population: 6,834,942

Area: 91,428 sq. mi
(236,800 sq. km)

Language: Lao, French, English,
ethnic languages

Currency: kip

Latvia
World Region: Europe

Capital: Riga

Population: 2,231,503

Area: 24,938 sq. mi
(64,589 sq. km)

Language: Latvian, Russian,
Lithuanian

Currency: Latvian lat

Lebanon
World Region: Middle East

Capital: Beirut

Population: 4,017,095

Area: 4,015 sq. mi
(10,400 sq. km)

Language: Arabic, French, English,
Armenian

Currency: Lebanese pound

Lesotho
World Region: Africa

Capital: Maseru

Population: 2,130,819

Area: 11,720 sq. mi (30,355 sq. km)

Language: Sesotho, English, Zulu, Xhosa

Currency: loti, South African rand

Liberia
World Region: Africa

Capital: Monrovia

Population: 3,441,790

Area: 43,000 sq. mi (111,370 sq. km)

Language: English, ethnic group languages

Currency: Liberian dollar

Libya
World Region: Africa

Capital: Tripoli

Population: 6,310,434

Area: 679,358 sq. mi (1,759,540 sq. km)

Language: Arabic, Italian, English

Currency: Libyan dinar

Liechtenstein
World Region: Europe

Capital: Vaduz

Population: 34,761

Area: 62 sq. mi (160 sq. km)

Language: German, Alemannic dialect

Currency: Swiss franc

Lithuania
World Region: Europe

Capital: Vilnius

Population: 3,555,179

Area: 25,174 sq. mi 65,200 sq. km)

Language: Lithuanian, Russian, Polish

Currency: litas

Luxembourg
World Region: Europe

Capital: Luxembourg

Population: 491,775

Area: 998 sq. mi (2,586 sq. km)

Language: Luxembourgish, German, French

Currency: euro

Macedonia
World Region: Europe

Capital: Skopje

Population: 2,066,718

Area: 9,781 sq. mi (25,333 sq. km)

Language: Macedonian, Albanian, Turkish

Currency: Macedonian denar

Madagascar
World Region: Africa

Capital: Antananarivo

Population: 20,653,556

Area: 226,656 sq. mi (587,040 sq. km)

Language: English, French, Malagasy

Currency: Malagasy franc

Malawi
World Region: Africa

Capital: Lilongwe

Population: 14,268,711

Area: 45,745 sq. mi (118,480 sq. km)

Language: Chichewa, Chinyanja, Chiyao, Chitumbuka

Currency: Malawian kwacha

Malaysia
World Region: Southeast Asia

Capital: Kuala Lumpur

Population: 25,715,819

Area: 127,316 sq. mi
(329,750 sq. km)

Language: Bahasa Malaysia,
English, Chinese, Tamil

Currency: ringgit

Maldives
World Region: Asia

Capital: Male

Population: 396,334

Area: 116 sq. mi
(300 sq km)

Language: Maldivian Dhivehi,
English

Currency: rufiyaa

Mali
World Region: Africa

Capital: Bamako

Population: 12,666,987

Area: 478,764 sq. mi
(1,240,000 sq km)

Language: French, Bambara,
African languages

Currency: CFA franc

Malta
World Region: Europe

Capital: Valletta

Population: 405,165

Area: 122 sq. mi
(316 sq. km)

Language: Maltese, English

Currency: euro

Marshall Islands
World Region: Oceania

Capital: Majuro

Population: 64,522

Area: 70 sq. mi
(181 sq. km)

Language: Marshallese, English

Currency: U.S. dollar

Mauritania
World Region: Africa

Capital: Nouakchott

Population: 3,129,486

Area: 397,953 sq. mi
(1,030,700 sq. km)

Language: Arabic, Pulaar, Soninke,
Wolof, French, Hassaniya

Currency: ouguiya

Mauritius
World Region: Africa

Capital: Port Louis

Population: 1,284,264

Area: 788 sq. mi
(2,040 sq. km)

Language: Creole, Bhojpuri,
French, English

Currency: Mauritian rupee

Mexico
World Region: North America

Capital: Mexico City

Population: 111,211,789

Area: 761,602 sq. mi
(1,972,550 sq. km)

Language: Spanish, indigenous
languages (Maya, Nahuatl)

Currency: Mexican peso

Micronesia
World Region: Oceania

Capital: Palikir

Population: 107,434

Area: 271 sq. mi
(702 sq. km)

Language: English, Chuukese,
Kosrean, Pohnpeian, Yapese

Currency: U.S. dollar

Moldova

World Region: Europe

Capital: Chisinau

Population: 4,320,748

Area: 13,067 sq. mi
(33,843 sq. km)

Language: Moldovan, Russian,
Gagauz

Currency: Moldovan leu

Monaco

World Region: Europe

Capital: Monaco

Population: 32,965

Area: 0.76 sq. mi
(1.95 sq. km)

Language: French, English,
Italian, Monegasque

Currency: euro

Mongolia

World Region: Asia

Capital: Ulaanbaatar

Population: 3,041,142

Area: 603,905 sq. mi
(1,564,116 sq. km)

Language: Khalkha Mongol,
Turkic, Russian

Currency: togrog/tugrik

Montenegro

World Region: Europe

Capital: Podgorica

Population: 672,180

Area: 5,415 sq. mi
(14,026 sq. km)

Language: Serbian,
Montenegrin, Bosnian, Albanian

Currency: euro

Morocco

World Region: Africa

Capital: Rabat

Population: 34,859,364

Area: 172,413 sq. mi
(446,550 sq. km)

Language: Arabic, Berber
dialects, French

Currency: Moroccan dirham

Mozambique

World Region: Africa

Capital: Maputo

Population: 21,669,278

Area: 309,494 sq. mi
(801,590 sq. km)

Language: Emakhuwa,
Xichangana, Portuguese, Elomwe,
Cisena, Echuwabo, others

Currency: metical

Myanmar (Burma)

World Region: Southeast Asia

Capital: Rangoon

Population: 48,137,741

Area: 261,969 sq. mi
(678,500 sq. km)

Language: Burmese, ethnic group
languages

Currency: kyat

Namibia

World Region: Africa

Capital: Windhoek

Population: 2,108,665

Area: 318,694 sq. mi
(825,418 sq. km)

Language: English, Afrikaans,
German

Currency: Namibian dollar,
South African rand

Nauru

World Region: Oceania

Capital: Yaren District

Population: 14,019

Area: 8 sq. mi
(21 sq. km)

Language: Nauruan, English

Currency: Australian dollar

Nepal
World Region: Asia

Capital: Kathmandu

Population: 28,563,377

Area: 54,363 sq. mi
(140,800 sq. km)

Language: Nepali, Maithali,
Bhojpuri, Tharu, Tamang, English

Currency: Nepalese rupee

The Netherlands
World Region: Europe

Capital: Amsterdam; The Hague

Population: 16,715,999

Area: 16,033 sq. mi
(41,526 sq. km)

Language: Dutch, Frisian

Currency: euro

New Zealand
World Region: OCeania

Capital: Wellington

Population: 4,213,418

Area: 103,737 sq. mi
(268,680 sq. km)

Language: English, Maori, Sign
Language

Currency: New Zealand dollar

Nicaragua
World Region: Central America

Capital: Managua

Population: 5,891,199

Area: 49,998 sq. mi
(129,494 sq. km)

Language: Spanish, Miskito

Currency: gold cordoba

Niger
World Region: Africa

Capital: Niamey

Population: 15,306,252

Area: 489,189 sq. mi
(1,267,000 sq. km)

Language: French, Hausa, Djerma

Currency: CFA franc

Nigeria
World Region: Africa

Capital: Abuja

Population: 149,229,090

Area: 356,667 sq. mi
(923,768 sq. km)

Language: English, Hausa,
Yoruba, Igbo, Fulani

Currency: naira

Norway
World Region: Europe

Capital: Oslo

Population: 4,660,539

Area: 125,181 sq. mi
(324,220 sq. km)

Language: Bokmal Norwegian,
Nynorsk Norwegian, Sami

Currency: Norwegian krone

Oman
World Region: Middle East

Capital: Muscat

Population: 3,418,085

Area: 82,031 sq. mi
(212,460 sq. km)

Language: Arabic, English,
Baluchi, Urdu, Indian dialects

Currency: Omani rial

Pakistan
World Region: Asia

Capital: Islamabad

Population: 176,242,949

Area: 310,401 sq. mi
(803,940 sq. km)

Language: Punjabi, Sindhi, Siraiki,
Pashtu, Urdu, English

Currency: Pakistani rupee

Palau
World Region: Oceania

Capital: Koror

Population: 20,796

Area: 177 sq. mi
(458 sq. km)

Language: Palauan, English,
Sonsoralese, Tobi, Angaur,
Filipino, Chinese

Currency: U.S. dollar

Panama
World Region: Central America

Capital: Panama

Population: 3,360,474

Area: 30,193 sq. mi
(78,200 sq. km)

Language: Spanish, English

Currency: balboa

Papua New Guinea
World Region: Oceania

Capital: Port Moresby

Population: 6,057,263

Area: 178,703 sq. mi
(462,840 sq. km)

Language: Tok Pisin, English,
Hiri Motu, approx. 860 indigenous
languages

Currency: kina

Paraguay
World Region: South America

Capital: Asuncion

Population: 6,995,655

Area: 157,046 sq. mi
(406,750 sq. km)

Language: Spanish, Guarani

Currency: guarani

Peru
World Region: South America

Capital: Lima

Population: 29,546,963

Area: 496,223 sq. mi
(1,285,220 sq. km)

Language: Spanish, Quechua,
Aymara, Amazonian languages

Currency: nuevo sol

Philippines
World Region: Southeast Asia

Capital: Manila

Population: 97,976,603

Area: 115,830 sq. mi
(300,000 sq. km)

Language: Filipino, English,
dialects

Currency: Philippine peso

Poland
World Region: Europe

Capital: Warsaw

Population: 38,482,919

Area: 120,728 sq. mi
(312,685 sq. km)

Language: Polish

Currency: zloty

Portugal
World Region: Europe

Capital: Lisbon

Population: 10,707,924

Area: 35,672 sq. mi
(92,391 sq. km)

Language: Portuguese,
Mirandese

Currency: euro

Qatar
World Region: Middle East

Capital: Doha

Population: 833,285

Area: 4,416 sq. mi
(11,437 sq. km)

Language: Arabic, English

Currency: Qatari rial

Romania

World Region: Europe

Capital: Bucharest

Population: 22,215,421

Area: 91,699 sq. mi (237,500 sq. km)

Language: Romanian, Hungarian

Currency: lei

Russia

World Region: Europe and Asia

Capital: Moscow

Population: 140,041,247

Area: 6,592,735 sq. mi (17,075,200 sq. km)

Language: Russian, minority languages

Currency: Russian ruble

Rwanda

World Region: Africa

Capital: Kigali

Population: 10,473,282

Area: 10,169 sq. mi (26,338 sq. km)

Language: Kinyarwanda, Bantu vernacular, French, English, Kiswahili

Currency: Rwandan franc

Saint Kitts and Nevis

World Region: The Caribbean

Capital: Basseterre

Population: 40,131

Area: 101 sq. mi (261 sq. km)

Language: English

Currency: East Caribbean dollar

Saint Lucia

World Region: The Caribbean

Capital: Castries

Population: 160,267

Area: 238 sq. mi (616 sq. km)

Language: English, French patois

Currency: East Caribbean dollar

Saint Vincent and the Grenadines

World Region: The Caribbean

Capital: Kingstown

Population: 104,574

Area: 150 sq. mi (389 sq. km)

Language: English, French patois

Currency: East Caribbean dollar

Samoa

World Region: Oceania

Capital: Apia

Population: 219,998

Area: 1,137 sq. mi (2,944 sq. km)

Language: Samoan (Polynesian), English

Currency: tala

San Marino

World Region: Europe

Capital: San Marino

Population: 30,324

Area: 24 sq. mi (62 sq. km)

Language: Italian

Currency: euro

São Tomé and Príncipe

World Region: Africa

Capital: São Tomé

Population: 212,679

Area: 386 sq. mi (1,001 sq. km)

Language: Portuguese

Currency: dobra

Saudi Arabia
World Region: Middle East

Capital: Riyadh

Population: 28,686,633

Area: 756,981 sq. mi
(1,960,582 sq. km)

Language: Arabic

Currency: Saudi riyal

Senegal
World Region: Africa

Capital: Dakar

Population: 13,711,597

Area: 75,749 sq. mi
(196,190 sq. km)

Language: French, Wolof, Pular,
Jola, Mandinka

Currency: CFA franc

Serbia
World Region: Europe

Capital: Belgrade

Population: 7,379,339

Area: 39,517 sq. mi
(102,350 sq. km)

Language: Serbian, Hungarian,
Bosniak

Currency: new Yugoslav dinar,
euro

Seychelles
World Region: Africa

Capital: Victoria

Population: 87,476

Area: 176 sq. mi
(455 sq. km)

Language: Creole, English

Currency: Seychelles rupee

Sierra Leone
World Region: Africa

Capital: Freetown

Population: 6,440,053

Area: 27,699 sq. mi
(71,740 sq. km)

Language: English, Mende,
Temne, Krio

Currency: leone

Singapore
World Region: Southeast Asia

Capital: Singapore

Population: 4,657,542

Area: 267 sq. mi
(692 sq. km)

Language: Mandarin, English,
Malay, Hokkien, Cantonese

Currency: Singapore dollar

Slovakia
World Region: Europe

Capital: Bratislava

Population: 5,463,046

Area: 18,859 sq. mi
(48,845 sq. km)

Language: Slovak, Hungarian

Currency: Slovak koruna

Slovenia
World Region: Europe

Capital: Ljubljana

Population: 2,005,692

Area: 7,827 sq. mi
(20,273 sq. km)

Language: Slovenian, Serbo-
Croatian

Currency: euro

Solomon Islands
World Region: Oceania

Capital: Honiara

Population: 393,613

Area: 10,985 sq. mi
(28,450 sq. km)

Language: Melanesian pidgin,
English, 120 indigenous
languages

Currency: Solomon Islands dollar

Somalia
World Region: Africa

Capital: Mogadishu

Population: 9,832,017

Area: 246,199 sq. mi (637,657 sq. km)

Language: Somali, Arabic, Italian, French

Currency: Somali shilling

South Africa
World Region: Africa

Capital: Pretoria (administrative), Cape Town (legislative), Bloemfontein (judicial)

Population: 49,052,489

Area: 471,008 sq. mi (1,219,912 sq. km)

Language: IsiZulu, IsiXhosa, Afrikaans, Sepedi, English, Setswana, Sesotho

Currency: rand

Spain
World Region: Europe

Capital: Madrid

Population: 40,525,002

Area: 194,896 sq. mi (504,782 sq. km)

Language: Castilian Spanish, Catalan, Galician, Basque

Currency: euro

Sri Lanka
World Region: Asia

Capital: Colombo

Population: 21,324,791

Area: 25,332 sq. mi (65,610 sq. km)

Language: Sinhala, Tamil, English

Currency: Sri Lankan rupee

Sudan
World Region: Africa

Capital: Khartoum

Population: 41,087,825

Area: 967,493 sq. mi (2,505,810 sq. km)

Language: Arabic, English, Nubian, Ta Bedawie, dialects

Currency: Sudanese dinar

Suriname
World Region: South America

Capital: Paramaribo

Population: 481,267

Area: 63,039 sq. mi (163,270 sq. km)

Language: Dutch, English, Sranang Tongo, Caribbean Hindustani, Javanese

Currency: Surinamese dollar

Swaziland
World Region: Africa

Capital: Mbabane

Population: 1,123,913

Area: 6,704 sq. mi (17,363 sq. km)

Language: English, siSwati

Currency: lilangeni

Sweden
World Region: Europe

Capital: Stockholm

Population: 9,059,651

Area: 173,731 sq. mi (449,964 sq. km)

Language: Swedish, Sami, Finnish

Currency: Swedish krona

Switzerland
World Region: Europe

Capital: Bern

Population: 7,604,467

Area: 15,942 sq. mi (41,290 sq. km

Language: German, French, Italian, Romansch

Currency: Swiss franc

Syria
World Region: Middle East

Capital: Damascus

Population: 20,178,485

Area: 71,498 sq. mi
(185,180 sq. km)

Language: Arabic, Kurdish,
Armenian, Aramaic,
Circassian, French, English

Currency: Syrian pound

Taiwan
World Region: Asia

Capital: Taipei

Population: 22,974,347

Area: 13,892 sq. mi
(35,980 sq. km)

Language: Mandarin Chinese,
Taiwanese, Hakka dialects

Currency: new Taiwan dollar

Tajikistan
World Region: Asia

Capital: Dushanbe

Population: 7,349,145

Area: 55,251 sq. mi
(143,100 sq. km)

Language: Tajik, Russian

Currency: somoni

Tanzania
World Region: Africa

Capital: Dar es Salaam

Population: 41,048,532

Area: 364,898 sq. mi
(945,087 sq. km)

Language: Kiswahili. Kiunguja,
English, Arabic

Currency: Tanzanian shilling

Thailand
World Region: Southeast Asia

Capital: Bangkok

Population: 65,905,410

Area: 198,455 sq. mi
(514,000 sq. km)

Language: Thai, English,
ethnic and regional dialects

Currency: baht

Togo
World Region: Africa

Capital: Lome

Population: 6,019,877

Area: 21,925 sq. mi
(56,785 sq. km)

Language: French, Ewe, Mina,
Kabye, Dagomba

Currency: CFA franc

Tonga
World Region: Oceania

Capital: Nuku'alofa

Population: 120,898

Area: 289 sq. mi
(748 sq. km)

Language: Tongan, English

Currency: pa'anga

Trinidad and Tobago
World Region: The Caribbean

Capital: Port-of-Spain

Population: 1,229,953

Area: 1,980 sq. mi
(5,128 sq. km)

Language: English, Caribbean
Hindustani, French, Spanish,
Chinese

Currency: Trinidad and Tobago
dollar

Tunisia
World Region: Africa

Capital: Tunis

Population: 10,486,339

Area: 63,170 sq. mi
(163,610 sq. km)

Language: Arabic, French

Currency: Tunisian dinar

Turkey
World Region: Middle East

Capital: Ankara

Population: 76,805,524

Area: 301,382 sq. mi
(780,580 sq. km)

Language: Turkish, Kurdish,
minority languages

Currency: Turkish lira

Turkmenistan
World Region: Asia

Capital: Ashgabat

Population: 4,884,887

Area: 188,455 sq. mi
(488,100 sq. km)

Language: Turkmen, Russian,
Uzbek

Currency: Turkmen manat

Tuvalu
World Region: Oceania

Capital: Funafuti

Population: 12,373

Area: 10 sq. mi
(26 sq. km)

Language: Tuvaluan, English,
Samoan, Kiribati

Currency: Australian dollar,
Tuvaluan dollar

Uganda
World Region: Africa

Capital: Kampala

Population: 32,369,558

Area: 91,135 sq. mi
(236,040 sq. km)

Language: English, Ganda, Niger-
Congo languages, Nilo-Saharan
languages, Swahili, Arabic

Currency: Ugandan shilling

Ukraine
World Region: Europe

Capital: Kyiv (Kiev)

Population: 45,700,395

Area: 233,089 sq. mi
(603,700 sq. km)

Language: Ukrainian, Russian

Currency: hryvnia

United Arab Emirates
World Region: Middle East

Capital: Abu Dhabi

Population: 4,798,491

Area: 32,000 sq. mi
(82,880 sq. km)

Language: Arabic, Persian,
English, Hindi, Urdu

Currency: Emirati dirham

United Kingdom
World Region: Europe

Capital: London

Population: 61,113,205

Area: 94,525 sq. mi
(244,820 sq. km)

Language: English, Welsh,
Scottish form of Gaelic

Currency: British pound

United States
World Region: North America

Capital: Washington, D.C.

Population: 307,212,123

Area: 3,718,690 sq. mi
(9,631,418 sq. km)

Language: English, Spanish,
indo-European, Asian and
Pacific island, Hawaiian

Currency: U.S. dollar

Uruguay
World Region: South America

Capital: Montevideo

Population: 3,494,382

Area: 68,039 sq. mi
(176,220 sq. km)

Language: Spanish, Portunol

Currency: Uruguayan peso

Uzbekistan
World Region: Asia

Capital: Tashkent

Population: 27,606,007

Area: 172,741 sq. mi
(447,400 sq. km)

Language: Uzbek, Russian,
Tajik

Currency: Uzbekistani sum

Vanuatu
World Region: Oceania

Capital: Port-Villa

Population: 218,519

Area: 4,710 sq. mi
(12,200 sq. km)

Language: local languages,
pidgin (Bislama), English, French

Currency: vatu

Vatican City (Holy See)
World Region: Europe

Capital: Vatican City

Population: 826

Area: .17 sq. mi
(.44 sq. km)

Language: Italian, Latin, French

Currency: euro

Venezuela
World Region: South America

Capital: Caracas

Population: 26,814,843

Area: 352,143 sq. mi
(912,050 sq. km)

Language: Spanish, indigenous
dialects

Currency: bolivar

Vietnam
World Region: Southeast Asia

Capital: Hanoi

Population: 86,967,524

Area: 127,243 sq. mi
(329,560 sq. km)

Language: Vietnamese, English,
French, Chinese, Khmer

Currency: dong

Yemen
World Region: Middle East

Capital: Sanaa

Population: 23,822,783

Area: 203,849 sq. mi
(527,970 sq. km)

Language: Arabic

Currency: Yemeni rial

Zambia
World Region: Africa

Capital: Lusaka

Population: 11,862,740

Area: 290,584 sq. mi
(752,614 sq. km)

Language: Bemba, Nyanja,
Tonga, Lozi, Lunda, Kaonde,
Luvale, English

Currency: Zambian kwacha

Zimbabwe
World Region: Africa

Capital: Harare

Population: 11,392,629

Area: 150,803 sq. mi
(390,580 sq. km)

Language: English, Shona,
Sindebele, tribal dialects

Currency: Zimbabwean dollar

Index

Credits

Picture Credits

Unless specifically noted below, all photo images are the property of USA TODAY, all rights retained.

All illustrations by Andy Taray, Christy Taray, and Christian Woltman for Ohioboy Art & Design.

Quick Look: p. 10: Chesley Sullenberger: AP Photo/Jason DeCrow, File; Bernie Madoff: AP Photo/Louis Lanzano, File

Animals: pp. 15–18: all images: Shutterstock, except p. 17: Blue Whale: © Visuals Unlimited/Corbis; p. 19: Cat: Shutterstock; p. 21: Vegetables: Shutterstock

Body & Health: pp. 22–23: all images: Shutterstock; p.25: Food Pyramid: Copyright © 2008. For more information about The Healthy Eating Pyramid, please see The Nutrition Source, Department of Nutrition, Harvard School of Public Health, http://www.thenutritionsource.org, and *Eat, Drink, and Be Healthy*, by Walter C. Willett, M.D. and Patrick J. Skerrett (2005), Free Press/Simon & Schuster Inc.; p. 26: Chicken: Shutterstock; p. 28: Vitamins: Shutterstock; p. 29: Michelle Obama: Official White House Photo by Samantha Appleton

Environment & Weather: pp. 30–37: all images: Shutterstock, except p. 34: drought (USA TODAY).

Popular Culture: p. 45: Susan Boyle: AP Photo/Andrew Milligan, PA

Science & Technology: pp. 52–53: all images: Shutterstock; p. 54: all images: Library of Congress; p. 55: moon: Shutterstock; pp. 56–58: all images: Shutterstock; p. 59: Rover: Courtesy NASA/JPL-Caltech; Galileo, Hubble, and Apollo 11: NASA; p. 60: Hubble: NASA; p. 61: lab researcher: Shutterstock; pp. 64–65: Abacus and Floppy Discs: Shutterstock; p. 65: Nook: Courtesy of Barnes & Noble

Sports: p. 66: David Beckham: AP Photo/Nick Wass; p. 68: bog snorkeling: AP Photo/PA, David Jones; underwater hockey: AP Photo/Tom Uhlman

United States: p. 79: Library of Congress Geography and Map Division; p. 82: Clara Barton and Harriet Tubman: Library of Congress Prints and Photographs Division; p. 83: Michael J. Fox: AP Photo/Peter Kramer; p. 89: Lincoln: Library of Congress Prints and Photographs Division; p. 104–110: U.S. Presidents: Library of Congress Prints and Photographs Division, except p. 108: President John F. Kennedy: John F. Kennedy Presidential Library and Museum, Boston; p. 110: President George W. Bush: White House photo by Eric Draper, Courtesy of the George W. Bush Presidential Library; President Barack H. Obama: Official White House Photo by Pete Souza; First Ladies: Library of Congress Prints and Photographs Division, except Nancy Reagan, Hillary Clinton, Laura Bush, and Michelle Obama (USA TODAY)

World: pp. 112–119: maps: Library of Congress Geography and Map Division; p. 120: Helen Keller: Library of Congress Prints and Photographs Division; p. 121: Pocahontas: Library of Congress Rare Book Division; Susan B. Anthony: Library of Congress Prints and Photographs Division; p. 122: Nelson Mandela: AP Photo/Themba Hadebe, Pool; p. 123: Mozart: Library of Congress Rare Book Division; Pablo Picasso: AP Photo; p. 124: Magellan and Drake: Library of Congress Prints and Photographs Division; p. 125: Lewis and Clark: Independence National Historical Park; Sally Ride: AP Photo/NASA; pp. 126–147: Flags: Shutterstock

USA TODAY Writer Contributions

ANIMALS

DINOSAURS FOREVER, p. 16: contains references to *USA Today*, "Scientist says lots of dinosaurs remain," 9/5/2006, © 2007 The Associated Press, along with other material.

'ORDINARY' PETS TO THE RESCUE, p. 20: *USA Today*, "'Ordinary' pets to the rescue on human-animal therapy teams" by Sharon L. Peters, 4/30/2008 (abridged).

CHANGING THEIR LIVES FOR THE LOVE OF ANIMALS, p. 21: contains references to *USA Today*, "First count finds 1 in 200 kids are vegetarians," 1/11/2009, by Mike Stobber, © 2009 Associated Press.

BODY & HEALTH

HAVE YOU HEARD?, p. 26: from *USA Today*, "Obesity a key link to soaring health tab as costs double," by Nanci Hellmich, 7/28/2009 (abridged), which references a study published online in *Health Affairs*.

CREATE A HEALTHFUL ENVIRONMENT IN YOUR HOME, p. 26: *USA Today*, "Six tips for parents to create a healthful environment," 1/14/2008 (abridged).

POWER LUNCHES, p. 27: *USA Today*, "Easy and healthy school lunches? It's in the bag" by Nanci Hellmich, 8/25/2008 (abridged).

EXERCISE VIDEO GAMES, p. 28: *USA Today*, "Exercise video games get kids off the couch" by Erica R. Hendry, 7/30/2008 (abridged).

NEW WHITE HOUSE VEGGIE GARDEN, p. 29: *USA Today* articles "First lady breaks ground on White House veggie garden" and "Michelle Obama touts healthy eating as she tills new White House garden" by Janice Lloyd, 3/20/2009 (abridged and combined).

ENVIRONMENT & WEATHER

THE COLDEST WINTERS AND HOTTEST SUMMERS ON EARTH, p. 35: *USA Today* blog post from The Weather Guys answering the question "Where are the coldest winters—and the hottest summers—on Earth?" by Doyle Rice, 2/23/2009.

TORNADOES: EARTH'S MOST VIOLENT STORMS, p. 36: *USA Today*, "Tornadoes are Earth's most violent storms," 9/12/2006 (abridged).

WHAT MAKES A STORM A HURRICANE?, p. 37: *USA Today*, "What makes a storm a hurricane" by Chad Palmer.

UNDERSTANDING CLIMATE CHANGE, p. 37: *USA Today*, "Understanding Climate Change" (abridged).

DISNEY STARS GO GREEN, p. 39: *USA Today*, "Disney stars ask kids to go green" by Ann Oldenburg, 5/14/2009 (abridged).

POPULAR CULTURE
MILEY CYRUS: HANNAH MONTANA AND BEYOND, p. 44: *USA Today*, "For Miley Cyrus, it's been quite the climb to movies" by Marco R. della Cava, 4/8/2009 (abridged).

iCARLY, p. 48: *USA Today* blog post "TV Taste Test: I sample 'iCarly,' 'Pitchmen' and more by Whitney Matheson, 6/2/2009 (abridged).

THE WIMPY KID GETS KIDS READING, p. 49: *USA Today*, "'Wimpy Kid: Last Straw' opens another 'gateway' to reading by Bob Minzesheimer, 1/13/2009 (abridged).

THE STORY BEHIND TWITTER, p.51: *USA Today*, "Twitter has millions tweeting in public communication service by Jon Swartz, 5/26/2009 (abridged).

SCIENCE & TECHNOLOGY
THE AMAZING POWERS OF THE HUBBLE SPACE TELESCOPE, p. 60: *USA Today*, "Hubble mission 'brain surgery' in space" by Dan Vergano, 5/14/2009 (abridged).

A NEW ERA FOR STEM CELL RESEARCH, p. 61: *USA Today*, " Q&A: Stem cell study enters new era" by Dan Vergano, 3/9/2009 (abridged).

FLU PANDEMIC, p. 62: *USA Today*, "WHO declares first flu pandemic in 41 years" by Steve Sterberg, 6/12/2009 (abridged).

FLYING CAR TAKES OFF, p. 62: *USA Today* blog post "Flying Car Takes Off" by Michelle Kessler, 3/19/09 (abridged).

SPORTS
QUITE A TRIP!, p. 67: *USA Today*, "Calif. teen hailed as youngest to sail world solo" by Michael Winter, 7/16/2009 (abridged).

THE BIGGEST OF THE MAJOR LEAGUES, p. 67: *USA Today* blog post "Lakers No. 1 now, but of all time?" by Reid Cherner and Tom Weir, 6/16/209 (abridged).

JIMMIE JOHNSON MAKES NASCAR HISTORY, p. 71: *USA Today*, "Four-gone conclusion: Title fits Johnson for NASCAR history" by Nate Ryan, 11/23/2009 (abridged).

A NEW BASEBALL CLASSIC: *USA Today*, "New Yankee Stadium touches all bases, gives nod to history" by Mike Dodd, with Mel Antonen, Steve DiMeglio and Seth Livingstone contributing, 4/16/2009 (abridged).

THE MLS CUP, p. 73: *USA Today*, "After overtime, penalty kicks, Real Salt Lake wins MLS Cup" by Beau Dure, 11/23/2009 (abridged).

QUITE A GAME!, p. 75: *USA Today* article "Carolina reign: Heels dominate Mich. State, claim national title" by Marlen Garcia, 4/7/2009 (abridged).

UNITED STATES
THE VICTORY OF BARACK OBAMA, p. 81: *USA Today*, "Obama to supporters: 'This is your victory'" by Kathy Keily, 11/5/2008 (abridged).

KIDS MAKING A DIFFERENCE, p. 83: *USA Today*, "Boy, 11, on trek to help homeless kids" by Emily Bazar, 5/18/2009 (abridged), along with other material.

Web Sites Referenced
America's Library: Presidents (http://www.americaslibrary.gov/cgi-bin/page.cgi/aa/presidents); *Billboard* Music Charts (http://www.billboard.com); CIA World Factbook (https://www.cia.gov); Country Reports (http://www.countryreports.org/); CNN: Most Admired Companies (http://money.cnn.com); Disney X-Games (http://disney.go.com); ESPN (http://sports.espn.go.com); FactMonster (http://www.factmonster.com); Famous Explorers (http://www.elizabethan-era.org.uk/famous-explorers.htm) and (http://www.famousexplorers.net/page1.html); Forbes Celebrity 100 (http://www.forbes.com); Fox Sports (http://msn.foxsports.com); History of Computers (http://www.computerhistory.org/timeline/); Influential Scientists (http://www.adherents.com/people/100_scientists.html) and (http://inventors.about.com/library/blcoindex.htm); Inside Movies (http://insidemovies.moviefone.com); Internet Movie Database (http://www.imdb.com); NASA (http://solarsystem.nasa.gov/index.cfm); National Football League (http://www.nfl.com); National Geographic (http://nationalgeographic.com); Nick (http:// www.nick.com); Nielson Ratings (http://blog.nielsen.com/nielsenwire); Nutrition Source (http://www.hsph.harvard.edu/nutritionsource); Olympics (http://www.olympic.org); Oprah (http://www.oprah.com); *Scientific American* (http://www.scientificamerican.com); States (http://www.infoplease.com) and (http://www.50states.com/) and (http://www.nationsencyclopedia.com); Top 10 Lists (http://www.top10lists.com/); Treehugger: A Discovery Company (http://www.treehugger.com); Unusual Sports (http://bestofstupid.com/weird-unusual-sports/); **USA TODAY (www.usatoday.com)**; *Variety* (http://www.variety.com); Webby Awards (http://www.webbyawards.com); White House Official Site (http://www.whitehouse.gov); Wikipedia (http://en.wikipedia.org); World Almanac for Kids (http://www.worldalmanacforkids.com); World Wildlife Federation (http://www.worldwildlife.org/); World's Worst Disasters (http://across.co.nz/WorldsWorstDisasters.html)

THE HEALTHY EATING PYRAMID, p. 25: Copyright © 2008. For more information about The Healthy Eating Pyramid, please see The Nutrition Source, Department of Nutrition, Harvard School of Public Health, http://www.thenutritionsource.org, and *Eat, Drink, and Be Healthy*, by Walter C. Willett, M.D. and Patrick J. Skerrett (2005), Free Press/Simon & Schuster Inc.